THE NATURE OF MEN

OF MEN

Elements of Masculine Psychology

John Ashfield

Originally Published by:
Mid North Regional Health Service
Booleroo Centre, South Australia, 5482

———————————————

Graphic design: Green Pigeon Graphics – Johanna Evans

Acknowledgements

Editing
Cynthia Collins

Special thanks to **Stephen Toon** and **Jim Herbert** for their encouragement and support with this project.

Contents

List of Tables

Introduction

For too long what we have been given to understand about gender issues, men, and male behaviour has not derived so much from sound knowledge or intelligent debate as from the entrenched dogma of gender ideology.

Unfortunately, much current literature dealing with these issues likewise offers little illumination, because of the reluctance of many authors to depart from the politically correct status quo.

However, for those people who have the keen interest or professional responsibility to broaden their knowledge beyond the censored renditions of these important issues, much relevant research data is now available.

The purpose of this book is to bring into focus and point towards more useful ways of understanding men, male psychology, and gender relations.

In Part 1, a good deal of space is devoted to discussion of sex-specific differences in men's and women's characteristic ways of thinking, relating, and conducting their emotional lives – differences due to both biological and cultural influences. Some of the means by which manhood and the well-being of men and boys can be enhanced are also explored. Given the emphasis throughout on sex-specific differences, some important qualifications need to be borne in mind: firstly, on-average differences between men and women should never be interpreted as some kind of prohibition against anyone – regardless of gender, from entering a career or performing a role that is generally thought to be the province of the other gender; secondly, what may be observed about men and women at the group level may not necessarily be true of a particular individual. Consequently, whilst observations about sex-specific differences and gender serve as a useful 'rule of thumb', they should never be applied too rigidly to any individual.

On occasions, individuals may exhibit a cognitive and emotional orientation that more resembles the on- average profile of the opposite gender. This does not pose a problem; it simply requires that one apply observations of gender (even if typically of the opposite gender) fitting the individual being observed, regardless of their biological sex.

Part 2 explores and proposes some ways of thinking about how the current version of manhood – evident in our culture (and the basis of male role socialization), can be enhanced, and by what means boys and men can achieve a more successful transition from 'boy psychology' to 'man psychology'.

Throughout the book, summaries and charts are tabled which are intended to reflect the content of chapters in a simple and abbreviated form for quick and easy reference.

As indicated by the title, the book endeavors to explore some important elements of masculine psychology. And though by no means an exhaustive treatment of the subject, it will hopefully enable readers to become both better informed and more discerning about the literature in this area – much of which, though purporting to promote men's well-being, merely serves to reinforce the deficit image of men reflected in current gender ideology.

For those readers who work with men, or intend to do so, there are several principles I would like to propose here for consideration. Firstly, we should work with men, or accept a position of responsibility for the promotion of their health or welfare, only if we actually value men – and yes, also like men. Secondly, any practitioner working with men in a professional or human service capacity is obligated to strive to obtain the best available knowledge to inform their work. Lastly, work with men is best practised out of a commitment to gender equity: women and men are deserving of being valued and respected; seeking equity for men should be seen as inseparable from an insistence on equity for women.

John Ashfield
October, 2004

Part One

Acknowledging and Understanding Difference

Prologue

For decades the message we have been getting about men is that, compared with women, they are emotionally underdeveloped, deficient, or, at best, inept. Women's ways of relating, viewing the world, and conducting their emotional lives have been held up as a model for men to adopt. One author commenting on men went so far as to say:

> *Self-destruction is masculine, getting better is feminine.[1]*

These ideas have been popularised by a conspicuously anti-male form of feminism called Gender Feminism. The chief distinguishing feature of this kind of feminism (in contrast to some other forms of feminism) is its particular theory of Social Constructionism. This theory about gender and human relations is now such a widespread belief that it is often asserted as an unquestionable truth. Its basic ideas are that:

> *Men and women are the same by nature; biological sex and gender identity are separate domains.*
>
> *Gender and gender roles are socially/culturally constructed, and are the product of patriarchal male cultural narratives invented by men in order to control and oppress women.[2]*

These ideas have been developed into a broader raft of dogma which asserts that:

- If gender is socially constructed (and has nothing to do with biology) then gender roles are interchangeable.

- If gender roles are socially constructed they can be abolished.

- Because gender and gender roles are a male invention to control and oppress women, then masculinity (or masculine gender) can and should be abolished.

- The world would be free of male domination, the oppression of women, and would be a better place, if men were demasculinised and if men and society were feminised.

- Men are largely responsible for societal and interpersonal problems stemming from their traditional gender identity – masculinity.

- Men's chief weapon for controlling and oppressing women is violence.

- Men must be made to adopt a feminine model of emotionality and psychological functioning. Until they do, they should be considered emotionally underdeveloped and deficient compared with women.

Where did the theory of feminist social constructionism spring from? In 1935 an anthropologist called Margaret Mead published her study *Sex and Temperament in Three Primitive Societies*. In order to counter some of the rigid thinking about gender roles at that time, she exaggerated the degree to which one of the societies she studied (the Tchambuli) associated what we would call the masculine with women and the feminine with men.[3/4/5]
Unfortunately, this was willfully misread to suggest that there was now clear evidence that here was a society that had reversed gender roles; thus 'proving' that gender is not only interchangeable, but is wholly socially/culturally constructed.[6/7]

Feminist social constructionism was born. The trouble was that it was conceived out the union of exaggerated data and a willful misinterpretation. For the next fifty years Margaret Mead stated over one hundred times that her research had never found or proven any such thing, but to no avail. Numerous university introductory sociology textbooks still quote Margaret Mead's study as evidence for social constructionism.[8] That this is so, and that this idea is still taught in many university courses, and is dominant in the fields of education, health and the human services, is a sobering reminder of how ideological dogma can ride over the top of any science, evidence, or intelligent disconfirmation that gets in its way.

Despite remaining a popular theory (even amongst some academics) and still the most widely used basis for interpreting gender relations and men's issues (including by many prominent male authors of books about men), social constructionism was not only ill-conceived but has been found to be fundamentally flawed. In the light of abundant current biological and anthropological evidence, we now know that sex-specific abilities and behaviours are rooted in male and female biology. Moreover, 'all social systems conform to the limits imposed by this reality'.[9]

The reason why men and women tend to be drawn to and to occupy largely different institutional and role domains in society, and why they experience 'sexually differentiated socialisation, is not to cause or produce male or female qualities – physiology alone would suffice for that... societies conform their institutions and socialisation to the sexual directions set by physiological differentiation'.[10/11]

This should not be taken to mean that biology can ever be an excuse for inequitable discrimination. Nor can it justifiably be used to generally limit men's and women's options, but it does explain 'universal sexual differences in behaviour and institutions, where cultural and environmental explanations cannot'.[12]

To summarise, we are now able to say that 'biology is the fundamental originator of gender, with social conditioning reinforcing or limiting, refining and accentuating gender characteristics specific to particular cultural and environmental contexts'.[13]

Masculinity, far from being interchangeable with femininity or capable of being abolished (as Gender Feminists have tried to assert), refers to male specific 'biologically innate cognitive and emotional processes and capacities, and the male-specific abilities and behaviours they give rise to'.[14]

When masculinity is adapted to, shaped by, and made specific to a particular cultural and environmental setting by social learning and cultural conditioning, the effect or result (in adult males) is best described as Manhood. Manhood in any particular culture exhibits what is generally considered to be manly or manliness.[15]

Close consideration of these phenomena – *masculinity* and *manhood* (and their supporting data), reveals insights about men's and women's comparative ways of conducting their emotional lives quite contrary to the 'politically correct' view most commonly held. We discover not the alleged male (compared with female) deficiency – instead, real and important *difference;* nor the much publicised male (compared with female) ineptitude – rather, a largely biologically determined and culturally demanded *aptitude.*

As will become evident from a range of research data, men and women exhibit (on average) important and necessary differences in how they conduct their emotional lives and communication, and in their preferred coping orientations, styles and strategies, consistent with biological and cultural imperatives.

As will also be shown, both women and men exhibit their own characteristic ways of *not coping,* through certain behaviours, and mental and emotional processes, that are dysfunctional and maladaptive. And though the focus here will be on men, it needs to be equally emphasised that both women and men benefit from efforts at improving self-insight, social and emotional conduct; both benefit from understanding that preferences of emotionality, communication, intimacy and ways of relating, rather than being a legitimate basis for pointing out each other's perceived shortcomings, are more the evidence of differences – differences that must be brought into an agreeable and workable dynamic tension.

1

Men and Emotions

Emotions are central to human life; and, just as they are deeply rooted in our biology and culture, their display is governed by a complex inter-relationship between our sex-specific (male or female) biology and the cultural rules and norms that dictate gender roles and expectations.[16]

All cultures determine to some degree the kind of emotional experiences and expression that are considered appropriate for males and females.[17] This relates closely to the kind of roles society demands that men and women perform – not only for survival, through the replication of society's essential primary structures (those which preserve family, production, safety, social order and governance), but also to maintain the kind of quality of life that society has come to expect.[18]

How and why emotions are learned, expressed or regulated (which includes self-regulation) also depends on one's worldview – that is, the overall perspective from which one sees and interprets the world. But again, such a worldview is not independent (nor can it be) of our sex-specific ways of constructing reality in our heads, or the social conditioning of culture.[19]

Just as emotions are a reflection of one's worldview, involving expressions of judgements and interpretations, they are as well both *somatic* (of, relating to and affecting the body), and *cognitive* (of, relating to and affecting the mind).

How effectively each of us interacts with one another socially, or with our physical environment, and how well we cope with life's challenges and potentially traumatising events (such as bereavement, illness, natural disasters and so on), also depends on the particular (sex-specific) strategies we use to manage and regulate our emotions.

EMOTION LANGUAGE AND KNOWLEDGE

It is well known that women use more emotion language – and with more variety and complexity than do men.

We now know that females, on average, have superior linguistic ability compared with males. This is thought to be partly attributable to a 'higher concentration of left brain linguistic functions and more reliance on the right hemisphere'.[20] This may also explain why females exhibit a superior capacity for learning complex grammatical constructions, and why school age girls 'tend to outperform boys in spelling, capitalisation, punctuation and comprehension of both spoken and written language'.[21] Greater interaction with the right hemisphere in female brains (thus enhancing scope for linguistic representations) would also appear to explain the appreciable difference between the sexes in associational fluency.[22] Though it has been found that the vocabularies of men and women are generally the same, males, on average:

> *...seem less adept at uncovering subtle nuances and connections in the meanings of words. Women on average are also dramatically better than men in "expressional fluency", or in generating sentences that illustrate grammatical rules.[23]*

Though most men are less verbally expressive than women, this does not mean that they are unfeeling; in men, emotion is more local to the right hemisphere, which has been found to collaborate less with the verbal capacities of the left hemisphere (compared with women). This reflects a functional difference rather than a behavioural deficit. As we will see, men simply utilise strategies that fit their sex-specific biological 'hardwiring' and cognitive orientation, suited largely to the roles they are predisposed to gravitate towards and are expected to perform.[24]

Not surprisingly, researchers have observed differences in emotion 'knowledge' (the capacity for awareness, discrimination, interpretation and prediction of emotion) in women compared to men. How women apply language to emotional experience may depend on available emotion knowledge. Women may have more 'elaborated knowledge structures'; alternatively, though men and women may have equally complex emotion knowledge, women may have greater access to this knowledge, because they both use what they know more frequently, and are willing and motivated to do so, because they have greater interest in the task.[25]

Women appear to be able to make use of their emotion knowledge to often better predict their own or other's feelings in a given situation than do men.[26] And women appear to have 'more differentiated emotion knowledge structures'.[27] When it comes to day-to-day experiences and recalling previous life experiences, again women exhibit a more 'elaborated view of their emotional lives'. Not only so, but their memory of emotional events, daily events in general – and the speed with which they can recall them, appears to be superior to men, because they 'encode and organise their autobiographical memories with more detail' and into a 'wider range of subjective categories'.[28]

One might expect women to display these preferences and capacities (and give attention to cues and encoding information of events), given their keener interest in day-to-day experiences and events, and the significance they attach to them. It is arguable that, even if men could do similarly, 'their default tendency may be not to attend to emotion cues to as great an extent'.[29]

Men are more likely to exhibit their emotional experiences in terms that are *action* oriented, because they are much more behaviourally oriented in their emotional expression than are women. Women tend also to be facially and verbally expressive in manifesting their 'greater conscious experience'.[30] And whilst women most often use complex verbal expression to represent their experience, and use self-reflective and conscious coping strategies dependent on language, men often prefer to regulate their emotions in an automatic behavioural fashion.[31]

Again, these two different sex-specific orientations or emphases, where women favour emotional expression and verbal expressiveness whereas men tend to favour action, action language and more automatic emotion regulation, fit with what we know about sex-specific differences in male/female brain functions.

Because the male brain tends to construct reality:

> ......in terms of abstract solutions and sequential movements in map space, men probably perceive action as more commensurate with their sense of the real. If action in the reality of males seems more "actual" than talking, this could explain, in part, why men are more inclined to associate intimacy with shared activities.[32]

That reality tends to be constructed this way in the male brain, favouring action over verbal expression, explains why males also tend to favour action metaphors in describing feelings. And that 'these constructions are probably less infused with feelings...could explain...why men have more difficulty talking about feelings'.[33/34] That women perceive conversation or talking as more expressive of emotions than action is also understandable, in view of their capacity for linguistic constructions of reality based on a broader range of data, available due to 'more extensive and interrelated cognitive and emotional contexts'.[35] For women:

> ....*the real could be more closely associated with language. This could be why women favour "rapport talk", or conversations about the personal and the private. If this talk is more commensurate with the actual character of reality in the female brain, women might depend on conversation to reinforce their reality more than men.*[36]

In contrast to men, women's linguistic constructions of reality tend to be much more infused with feelings (derivative of a much broader range of emotional 'data'), and women exhibit much less difficulty 'disclosing, describing, and contextualizing feelings'.[37/38]

Women's more elaborate and expressive emotion faculty, when applied to coping, does appear to have its drawbacks, although this should be understood in the context of the sex-specific roles that women gravitate towards and are generally expected to perform. The (on average) female copying style, which involves reflective language based emotion regulation, may tend to prolong negative emotional experiences. The female tendency to cope with emotion through rumination is thought to be a major reason why they are at higher risk of depressive illness, and experience more negative emotions than do men.[39/40]

Community-based epidemiological studies have shown that women exhibit almost twice the rate of clinical depression

---

Features of the On-average Female Emotion Faculty

- Women exhibit more differentiated emotion knowledge structures than do men.

- Have better memory and speedier recall of emotional experiences.

- Have a more elaborated view of their emotional lives.

- Exhibit linguistic constructions more infused with feelings based on a more available and broad range of emotion/experience/memory data.

- Give evidence of greater conscious emotional experience.

- Have a more elaborate capacity for emotional expression.

- Use reflective language based emotion regulation, which has been found to prolong emotional experience.

- Have a tendency to adopt a conscious ruminative coping style, dwelling on problems, their perceived cause, and the negative emotions associated with both (which may in some situations contribute to feelings of powerlessness, psychological strain, and the experience of depression); whereas men generally prefer to divert their attention away from the reasons for negative emotions and the negative emotions themselves, in an automatic behavioural fashion, consequenting apparently less intense, prolonged and debilitating emotional experience.

Table 1

compared to men.[41] Furthermore, evidence also suggests that, on average, women report higher levels of psychological strain than do men.[42]

A *ruminative* style of coping distinguishes women from men as a consistent cognitive gender based difference.[43] This tendency to dwell on a problem, its perceived cause, and the negative emotions associated with both, readily lends itself to a self-defeating cycle that can produce feelings of powerlessness and depressive symptoms – which in turn lead to more rumination, consequenting more problematical depression.

In contrast to this style of coping, men have been shown to prefer to engage in activities that help divert attention away from both the reasons for negative emotions and the negative emotions themselves.[44] This appears to be a comparably more adaptive and helpful response than the ruminative one.

A further gender-based cognitive difference that may help explain why women fare more poorly than men in their experience of negative affect, has to do with their tendency (more so than men) to feel that they are powerless to change situations that are anxiety producing.[45] In their cognitive processing, women are more likely than men to have a tendency to discount their successes and personalise their failures – as well as attributing success to luck or other external factors outside their control – thus enhancing their vulnerability to depression.[46/47]

EMOTION EXPERIENCE AND INTENSITY

We know that men are less emotionally expressive than women, and that women appear to have a more elaborate emotion faculty, but does this mean that men and women experience emotion differently – such as with more or less intensity? This is a difficult question. Because of the different methods used to research this issue, there is no clear consensus.

Early studies suggested that women tend to feel and articulate emotions at a generally greater level of intensity than men. Whether happiness or, conversely, emotions such as fear, sadness or anxiety, women were found to experience them more intensely than men.[48]

Cultural 'display-rules' and societal norms were proposed as having a significant influence, in that men are typically discouraged from the experience and public display of most emotions, whereas women are allowed much more latitude in their experience and public display of both positive and negative emotions.[49]

Another explanation was that differences in emotional intensity between men and women are likely attributable to, or at least associated with, how men and women view interpersonal relationships: women view partner relationships in terms of emotional intimacy; whereas men have expectations of companionship and camaraderie. If the relationship goes badly, again women (with their greater investment in the interpersonal aspects of the relationship) experience greater intensity of negative emotions than do men.[50]

More recent research focussing on emotional responses and expressivity, distinguishes emotional *impulse* intensity (an intense feeling prompting/suggesting a particular behaviour) from general emotional intensity. When compared with men, women were found to experience greater emotional impulse intensity, and more positive and negative expression of emotion. Men characteristically tended to mask their emotions.[51] Interestingly, when it came to expressive confidence, there was no reported difference between men and women[52] – suggesting that, rather than having a lack of confidence in expressing their feelings, men simply contain and limit expressive displays. Neither did women report experiencing more emotion than men – despite being more emotionally expressive – suggesting that, though cultural conditioning may contribute to greater emotional expressivity in women, it appears not to necessarily affect men's capacity to experience emotions.[53] Contrary to this inference, other research using electromyogram readings indicates that, when men and women are exposed to the same stimuli, women do indeed experience greater emotional intensity.[54]

One final observation worth noting from a summation of research about *sex differences in emotion*, is that the level of experienced emotional intensity may be higher for men than for women before it corresponds with emotional expression.[55]

Returning to our original question: Do men and women experience emotion differently – such as with more or less intensity? Though there is a resounding consensus that there are notable differences in emotional expressiveness between men and women, some disparity is apparent with regard to difference in *experience.* Some research indicates no clear difference between men's and women's reported experience, whereas other research indicates a significant difference in physiological activity and experienced emotional intensity, with women measuring higher scores for both positive and negative emotions. Though these differences can be accounted for by differences in the methods used to assess emotional experience, they serve to highlight the need for caution in making conclusive assertions. However, if we consider our observations of *Emotion language and knowledge* (see table 1), indicating a more elaborate on-average female emotional faculty compared with the on-average male, it is very likely that, though men may experience the same range of emotions as women, *in general* it is likely that women experience emotions with more conscious awareness, with greater intensity (including impulse intensity), and with better subsequent memory and speed of recall, than men. Though it should be noted that this capacity, experience, and associated preferred coping style (which tends to be ruminative, conscious, and language based), appears to contribute to more prolonged and debilitating negative emotional experience.

EMOTION EXPRESSION AND CONTEXT

An important question to pose about men and emotions is: Though men appear to be generally less emotionally expressive than women, are there particular settings in which this significantly varies? Research in relation to gender-emotion stereotypes and context suggests that the degree to which men and women express emotions (which are commonly taken to indicate how 'emotional' men or women are) depends on whether they are in what is generally considered to be their *domain*. For example, women are not expected to be more emotionally expressive than men in all situations, but in the context of interpersonal relations they are, because that is considered a women's domain. Men likewise are likely to be more expressive of the emotion they experience in the domain that is traditionally male.[56] The traditional male domain includes: predominantly male workplaces (places of production), competitive environments (including where competitive sport is played), male only groups and institutions, and environments where men are responsible for exercising control, mastery or governance, or in which men must concern themselves with the protection of family, community or country.

The only exception to this domain-specific emotional expression appears to be the expression of anger. Men are expected (and are therefore given licence) to be expressive of anger, irrespective of the gender delineated context which applies to other emotions. Women, on the other hand, are expected to be inexpressive of anger, regardless of context.[57]

Anger is in fact an exception for another reason. Though its expression does appear to be generally governed by 'gender delineated context', observational research of couple's patterns of communication indicates that wives disclose more hostile emotions than husbands.[58] When interviewed or observed in interactions, women have been found to express more anger than men.[59] Conflict research has also found that, in intimate relationships, women express more negative emotions than men.[60] There appears to be no pattern of greater expression of anger amongst men.[61] As we will see later, these findings are congruent with what we know about the most extreme manifestation of couple conflict – relationship violence.

These findings about emotion expression and context may have important implications for how we think about health and welfare service delivery environments and methods.

Generally these environments reflect a female/feminine culture. The majority of health and welfare personnel and users of services in these environments are female. Such environments are usually highly public, and have access, reception and waiting area arrangements and décor that are most suited to women and children. They also commonly display posters and literature addressing predominantly female and child health and welfare issues. The few messages targeting males are more often than not associated with violence, abuse, anger, or deficits in fathering. Despite such environments and services being funded by women *and* men (and often proudly articulating service imperatives of equality, accessibility, and sensitivity to consumer needs), we know that generally they are insensitive to male help-seeking behaviour, and discourage men and boys placing a much needed higher premium on their health. We also know that many males view these environments and some of their service delivery methods (environment also being method) as not only male unfriendly, but often inappropriate in nature, location, accessibility and convenience.[62/63/64/65]

If these service environments are perceived as a female 'domain', we might expect that men entering them for much needed services might experience anxiety (anxious arousal), due to being exposed to public attention in an environment strongly suggestive of unmanly weakness (due to exhibiting dependent behaviour – taking refuge amongst and with women) instead of manly independence and self-sufficiency. We might also expect that some men (already anxious, 'threatened' and embarrassed in such an environment), especially if they are kept waiting, could feel and likely express the emotion most contextually permissible – anger.

This may also shed some light on why, in environments with the potential to invite concentrations of mentally troubled individuals (whether or not a mental health service is offered), problems can occur. Anxious arousal and anger, combined with individual characteristics of poor impulse control, a pre-existing sense of powerlessness, or a personality with antisocial tendencies, may dysregulate an otherwise manageable male client, posing a potent and unnecessary risk to other people and, in the event of an incident, landing the client in trouble as well as likely disqualifying him from getting the kind of help or assistance that he needs.

This scenario may sound a touch melodramatic – except to those health and welfare workers who have not infrequently found themselves caught up in such a situation!

But what of ordinary untroubled male clients who have to enter these environments seeking assistance with matters whose resolution (such as with some personal health issues or a psychological one) depends on honest self-disclosure and honest emotional as well as cognitive engagement with a doctor, therapist, health or welfare worker? How well is the process likely to fare (and with what outcomes) in an environment so obviously a female domain – and one in which it is not 'permissible' to exhibit any emotion but anger? How likely is a male client showing signs of being angry to get a fair hearing or a good service (and all the more so in some couple counselling) where subtle emotions enlist support and elicit sympathy, but angry feelings are perceived as repellent and threatening, and may be mistakenly (and naïvely) taken to indicate a person's greater responsibility for a problem?

There is little doubt that this has been a cause of great injustice and misconception in individual and couple counselling. It surely begs the question: Should anyone be permitted to counsel men – let alone men and their partners – without a basic understanding of male and gender psychology? Recognition of anger: that it must be engaged, not ignored; utilised and resolved, not merely pathologised; and seen as a common emotional precursor behind which can be found a timid group of more subtle emotions, is but one elementary part of such an understanding.

As for service delivery environments, there is simply no excuse for them remaining unmodified in the knowledge that they are perceived by many men as 'user unfriendly'; nor can they (and the agencies and services they reflect) be excused for discouraging male users by making their access to and experience of services unnecessarily difficult and negative.

To conclude our observations about *emotion expression*

and context, what of the exception to domain specific emotional expression marked by women's anger in interpersonal relationships? We can say that health and welfare professionals would be well advised to bear this finding in mind when working with individual men – and especially when working with men and their partners – as a much needed counterpoise to the wrongful myth that men are more angry 'behind closed doors' than women (a topic we will explore further in subsequent discussion).

EMOTION, EXPRESSIVE SUPPRESSION AND MEMORY

As already noted in our observations about *Emotion Language and Knowledge*, women's memory of emotional events, and the speed with which they can recall them, appears to be superior compared with men's. Research specifically examining emotion regulation and memory suggests that the suppression of emotional expression (as a reaction to an emotional event) affects a person's memory of the emotional details of the event.[66] Because such expressive suppression requires expending mental energy on self-monitoring and self-correction, it is suggested that accuracy of verbal memory of the event (i.e. the ability to recall details associated verbally with the event) is consequently diminished.[67]

Expressive suppression has been found to expend similar cognitive resources, regardless of the intensity of the emotions being experienced. The research also identified that diminished memory was *not* associated with emotional inexpressiveness if a person used a form of cognitive reappraisal: that is, if they adopted a more detached interest in the event, and sought to reframe or reconstruct it in such a way as to modify its meaning – such as seeing it as a challenge rather than a threat.[68]

It would appear then that the verbal details associated with an emotional event may be harder to recall if one uses expressive suppression. However, when associated with some detached reappraisal of the event – thus modifying its threat or negative meaning – memory of the verbal details has been found to remain unimpaired.[69]

There is no doubt that expressive suppression is an essential part of any person's coping repertoire. Everyone will have the need to disguise their feelings on occasions. Men certainly do (as will be discussed in more detail later). And, whilst it may be a disadvantage to resolving a past conflict or negative interpersonal exchange if memory of the detail is poor, in many other instances, where the emotional content of events could prove to be overwhelming with too much memory, it could be a significant and life preserving advantage. This is particularly important for a person whose role demands ongoing protective vigilance towards others, affording little opportunity for a more passive ruminative posture.

The regulative strategies each of us uses in relation to our emotions will always tend to be largely sex-specific, because of our biological mental functioning and orientation, and because of corresponding normative cultural expectations and the kind of roles we perform. The idea that 'letting it all hang out' should be a preferred model of emotional conduct is perhaps as potentially dangerous as it is glib.

Women and men doubtless can benefit from adeptness in their use of a range of emotion management strategies, but this will always and ever be influenced by biological and cultural imperatives.

References

1.   Goldberg, H., **The New Male** (New York, William Morrow and Company, 1979) back jacket

2.   Nadeau, R., **She/He Brain: Science Sexual Politics And The Myths of Feminism** (U.S.A. Praeger, 1996) chapter 1

3.   Goldberg, S., **Feminism Against Science** *National Review*, November 18, 1991

4.   Wood, P., **Pacifist Hoax** (FrontPageMagazine.com September 12, 2003)

5.   See also, critiques of Mead's research:

      Freeman, D., **Margaret Mead and Samoa: The Making and Unmaking of an Anthropological Myth** (books issued on demand, supplier unknown, 1983), and, Roscoe, P., **Margaret Mead, Reo Fortune, and Mountain Arapesh Warfare** *American Anthropologist* 105 (3), 2003, pp. 581-591

6.   Op. cit., Goldberg, S., 1991

7.   Op. cit., Roscoe

8.   Op. cit., Goldberg, S., 1991

9.   Ibid.

10.   Goldberg, S., **The Inevitability of Patriarchy** (New York, William Morrow, 1973) p. 118

11.   For a more comprehensive treatment of this subject refer to: Ashfield, J., **Gender, Masculinity and Manhood: Core Concepts for Understanding Men's Issues** (Western Australia, Ikon Institute, 2003). *This*

book has been revised and reissued under the title:
The Making Of A Man: Reclaiming masculinity and manhood in the light of reason *(South Australia, Peacock Publications, 2004)*

12. Op. cit., Goldberg, 1973

13. Op. cit., Ashfield, 2003

14. Ibid.

15. Ibid.

16. Harre, R. and Parrott, W., **The Emotions: Social Cultural and Biological Dimensions** (London, Sage Publications, 2000) pp. 1-3

17. Ibid., p. 89

18. Gilmore, D., **Manhood In The Making** (U.S.A Yale University Press, 1990)

19. Op. cit., Nadeau

20. Ibid., p. 53

21. Ibid.

22. Op. cit., Ashfield, p. 83

23. Op. cit., Nadeau, p. 54

24. Op. cit., Ashfield, p. 85

25. Barrett, L., Lane, R., Sechrest, L., Schwartz, G., **Sex Differences in Emotional Awareness** *(Personality and Social Psychology Bulletin,* Vol. 26 No. 9, 2000) pp. 1027-1035

26. Ibid.

27. Ibid.

28. Ibid.

29. Ibid.

30. Ibid.

31. Ibid.

32. Op. cit., Nadeau, pp. 88 & 89

33. Ibid.

34. Op. cit., Ashfield, p. 96

35. Ibid.

36. Op. cit., Nadeau, pp. 86 & 89

37. Op. cit., Ashfield, p.97

38. Op. cit., Nadeau, pp. 86 & 89

39. Op. cit., Barrett et al.

40. Fujita, F., Diener, E., Sandvik, E., **Gender Differences in Negative Affect And Well-being: The Case For Emotional Intensity** *Journal of Personality And Social Psychology*, 1991, pp. 61, 427-434

41. Nolen-Hoeksema, S., **Sex Differences In Unipolar Depression: Evidence and Theory** *Psychological Bulletin*, 1987, pp. 101, 259-282

42. Jick, T. and Mitz, L., **Sex Differences In Work Stress.** *Academy of Management Review,* 1985, pp. 10, 408-442

43. Nolen-Hocksema, S., Larson, J., Grayson, L., **Explaining The Gender Differences In Depressive Symptoms** *Journal of Personality And Social Psychology*, 1999, pp. 77, 1061-1072

44. Op. cit., Jick & Mitz, 1985

45. Op. cit., Nolen-Hoeksema, 1987

46. Deaux, K., **Self-Evaluations of Male and Female Managers** *Sex Roles*, 1979, pp. 5, 571-580

47. Seligman, M., **Helplessness: On Depression Development and Death** (San Francisco, USA, Freeman, 1975)

48. Diener, E., Sandvik, E., Larson, R., **Age And Sex Effects For Emotional Intensity** *Developmental Psychology*, 1985, pp. 21, 542-546

49. Ibid.

50. Ibid.

51. Gross, J. and John, O., **Mapping The Domain Of Expressivity: Multimethod Evidence For A Hierarchical Model** *Journal of Personality And Social Psychology*, 1998, pp. 74, 170-191

52. Ibid.

53. Ibid.

54. Dimberg, U. and Lunguist, L., **Gender Differences In Facial Reactions To Facial Expressions** *Biological Psychology*, 1990, pp. 30, 151-159

55. Kring, A. and Gordon, A., **Sex Differences In Emotion: Expression, Experience and Physiology** *Journal of Personal and Social Psychology,* 1998, Vol. 74, No. 3, pp. 686-703

56. Kelly, J., **Gender-Emotion Stereotypes Are Context Specific** *Sex Roles: A Journal of Research*, 1999

57. Ibid.

58. Shimanoff, S., **The Role of Gender In Linguistic References To Emotive States** *Communication Quarterly*, 1983, pp. 31, 174-179

59. Dosser, D., Balswich, J., Halveston, D., **Situational Content Of Emotional Expressions** *Journal Of Counselling Psychology*, 1983, pp. 30, 375-387

60. Kelly, H., Cunningham, J., Grisham, J., Lefebvre, L., Sink, C., Yablon, G., **Sex Differences Made During Conflict Within Heterosexual Pairs** *Sex Roles*, 1978, pp. 4, 473-492

61. Op. cit., Dosser et al. 1983

62. Woods, M., **Men's Use of General Practitioner** *New South Wales Public Health Bulletin*, 2001, 12(12), pp. 334-335

63. Tudiver, F. and Talbot, Y., **Why Don't Men Seek Help? Family Physicians' Perspectives on Help-Seeking Behaviours in Men** *Journal of Family Practice*, 1999, 48(1), pp. 47-52

64. NSW Department of Health, **The Health of The People Of New South Wales – Report of The Chief Health Officer** (Sydney: NSW Department of Health, 2000)

65. Buckley, D. and Lower, T., **Factors Influencing The Utilisation of Health Services By Rural Men** *Australian Health Review*, 2002, Vol. 25, No.2, pp.11-15

66. Richards, J. and Gross, J., **Emotion Regulation and Memory: The Cognitive Cost of Keeping One's Cool** *Journal Of Personality and Social Psychology*, 2000, Vol. 79, No. 3

67. Ibid.

68. Ibid.

2

Men and Coping

Mention was made in the chapter about *Men and Emotions* of how men tend to be less verbally expressive of emotion than women, and use expressive suppression rather than rumination as a preferred regulatory strategy. Because suppression is a favoured and essential emotional management strategy for male role performance (in many though not all circumstances), and because it has been a target of those people who have sought to promote a deficit image of men and masculinity, it is needful that we examine it more closely.

The constant refrain of those who would demasculinise and feminise men is that 'men need to get in touch with their feelings'. Certainly, it is true that some men do become disconnected from their emotions (or at least appear to), just as some women get lost in their emotions, and experience deteriorating mental health as a consequence. Yet when we consider the imperatives of biology and culture, and male and female role demands, the sex-specific 'signature' coping styles (see table 2) of suppressive emotion regulation, and ruminative language based emotion regulation, make a whole lot of sense. Used appropriately they contribute inestimably to human well-being and survival. Employed with global rigidity they can cause serious problems.

It may be said then, that men's greatest gift sometimes is that they don't get in touch with their emotions! – that they are able to distance themselves from the emotional content of difficult, dangerous, and potentially overwhelming situations and events, in order to remain focussed, capable of immediate, decisive and problem solving action, to protect, defend, make safe, or bring order to chaos.

'Signature' (on-average) Coping Styles of Men and Women	
MEN	**WOMEN**
Suppression	Rumination
Behaviourally oriented in emotional expression	Verbally oriented in emotional expression
Exhibit emotional experiences in action oriented terms; often describe feelings with action metaphors	
Regulate emotion in an automatic behavioural fashion	Favour language based emotion regulation
The real tends to be more associated with action	The real tends to be closely associated with language; conversation is used to reinforce a sense of the real
Are inclined to associate intimacy with shared activities	Use shared activities as an opportunity for verbal intimacy

Table 2

Though this largely masculine aptitude may not be called upon in quite the same variety of dramatic ways as it has in the past, and though the luxury of our affluence appears in many ways to have diminished the need for traditional masculinity, men are still called upon to go to war, perform nearly all the dangerous, life threatening, and health diminishing dirty work of society, and must survive in the 'dog eat dog' competitiveness of the 'engine rooms' of construction, industry and production. It is demanded of them and, if not, it may be. And, as will be discussed later, the expectations of manhood alone demand a discipline and stoicism in men's emotional conduct which can only be dismissed at the peril of masculine gender identity. Even the new class of 'meterosexual' men, protected within the environs of urban affluence, must reckon with manhood; even if only to acknowledge that they are vicariously and practically dependant on other less privileged men for their precarious luxury.

SUPPRESSION AS A COPING STRATEGY

Before discussing suppression as a coping strategy, it is important to differentiate it from *repression,* though these terms are often (and inappropriately) used synonymously. Repression involves putting painful (or unacceptable) thoughts, memories and emotions out of mind and forgetting them. All psychological defences do this to some extent, but repression is *unconsciously* 'forgetting'; forgetting and not even realising it, and having no conscious memory or knowledge of the elements that have been repressed.[1]

Unlike repression, *suppression* is a conscious choice not to indulge a particular thought, feeling or memory. 'Not to indulge' means that though we may be aware of a thought or feeling, we decide neither to dwell on it (by internally continuing to think about it) nor to express it (by externally acting it out). We do this because a thought, emotion or impulse may not be helpful to the situation we find ourselves in, and/or because of time constraints in which 'we just can't deal with that right now'.

Suppression is a useful psychological mechanism which permits us to concentrate undistracted on what we are doing or on what needs to be done.[2] To be distracted by impulses, thoughts or emotions which arise, or to feel the need to act on them, could in many situations be unhelpful, hazardous or even dangerous.

Recent research into the relationship between suppressing negative emotions and mental health in adolescents revealed a significant sex-specific difference between male and female experience. It was found that if a person merely manipulates their behavioural output (by intentionally concealing and containing emotion) without an underlying 'attitude' or disposition that one *should* suppress one's emotions, little effect on mental health occurs.[3] This appears consistent with female internalised beliefs of gender socialisation and the biologically based on-average female cognitive orientation. Males who conceal and contain their emotions also tend to experience an associated *reduction* in the experience of emotions – including negative emotions – indicating a closer relationship between behaviour and attitude/disposition for males than females.[4] This appears to be consistent with male internalised beliefs of gender socialisation and the biologically based on-average male cognitive orientation.

The effects of this more characteristically male response (and therefore the utility of suppression) in relation to coping and mental health appear to be: a reduction in negative emotion/affect, because the diminished expression of emotions (like anger or sadness) also diminishes both the attention paid to them and the corresponding tendency to ruminate on them – reducing the strength and/or duration of these emotions; and/or perhaps a self-fulfilling prophecy, where a person unconsciously sets down an expectation and consequently (and unknowingly) behaves in a way consistent with and therefore in fulfilment of that expectation.[5]

As already mentioned, suppression will not always be an appropriate method for coping. Rumination is also important – such as in the process of gaining control over and insight into some stressful events, and for the reestablishment of a worldview that may have been shattered by a traumatic experience. Suppression used in these circumstances has the potential to cause a bottleneck effect – increasing the experience of negative emotions because they are constricted.[6]

Suppression as a regulator of thoughts and emotions appears in some circumstances to reduce both the experience and the verbal memory of negative emotional events. To be able to postpone and 'put on hold' certain thoughts, impulses and emotions in situations that demand a 'clear head', 'presence of mind' and detached decisive judgement and action is a huge asset. However, what can be a man's greatest strength can also be his greatest liability. Suppression does not mean *elimination*. There appears not to be a place in the human psyche into which unwanted emotional content can be discarded. Like a child ignored, such emotion may even gather energy and intensity (perhaps coalescing with other similar psychic content – such as seems to occur with grief) to exert disturbance or manifest somatic symptoms of a kind that will demand our attention.

If suppression results in verbal emotional inexpressiveness, and choosing not to indulge certain negative thoughts and emotions, instead putting them 'on hold' (until a threat or crisis has passed, order is restored, protective vigilance is no longer needed, a problem is solved, mastered or redefined in some satisfactory way), then it may also imply *a need to return* to what has been postponed (at an opportune time), to process and resolve it in some way. And, given the characteristic male emotional coping style, this may involve a form of emotional 'dosing': engaging turbulent, difficult or upsetting thoughts and emotions, 'taking a break' from them (to avoid being overwhelmed), and then returning once again to the task.

This of course is an over simplification of the complex issue of how and in what circumstances men may need to 'work through', in some way, the psychological effects of negative events. Doubtless, even following suppression, doing nothing consciously about 'lingering effects' of a negative event in many instances may be inconsequential because of the ingenuity of the human psyche to somehow resolve or absorb our many experiences through its myriad of inscrutable means. And yet we do know that the psychological/emotional sequelae due to *significant* emotional events such as trauma and bereavement, if postponed (and there is often good reason to do so), will likely need to be revisited and dealt with. For men, this reconnecting with 'material' put on hold will need to be timely – that is, when the individual is ready, and when it is permitted by there being an appropriately private and 'safe' environment in which to do so.

It is worth noting that trauma research indicates that following a traumatic event (with the potential to traumatise), immediately engaging negative thoughts and emotions, or attempting some kind of catharsis, may inhibit a needful (and adaptive) initial psychological *distancing* which allows for much needed social and solution oriented constructions to gain a stable focus.[7] It has been observed that people exposed to traumatic experiences appear to cope best if they can create some distance for themselves from the event and reframe, reconstrue or reappraise it – which is specifically contrary to the popular notion of early emotional venting.[8]

The *reconnecting* with and *working through* experience (thoughts and feelings) of a significant negative event will for men typically comprise the following elements:

Reflection/Solitude

To reflect on an event and one's experience of it is to 'make evident' its content and meaning. Reflection also entails 'mulling things over' and 'sizing them up'. Men often need solitude for this, which allows for safety away from the public gaze, and predisposes them to 'feeling experience'. Solitude, even in the course of daily work and activity, if it is away from others, can be a place where permission is available to be authentically oneself and to allow emotions/thoughts/experience to emerge and be expressed in a characteristically masculine way.

Reflection and solitude encourage thoughts to prompt and evoke feelings, and feelings to prompt and evoke thoughts. They give experience 'existence' and form, and provide the 'raw materials' for shaping a rational and adaptive perspective.

Action/Ritual

Men and action are synonymous. Men often deal with their emotion by using their strengths of action. Action consciously (or effectively) linked to emotions/thoughts/ experience can for men serve the same function (and achieve 'working through') as crying and verbal self-disclosure do for women.[9] This could be described as *ritualised action.* Historically, men have often used ritual to good effect. Ritual in the service of psychological/emotional healing, or 'working through', can provide the means by which to incrementally and safely engage painful experience – because such experience is contained within action and is expressed through it; neither suggesting weakness nor demanding a display of public vulnerability or dependence[10] – which, as we will see in our discussion of Men and Manhood, is vital to maintaining the integrity of the male gender self-identity. In an emotionally safe environment, men may well cry tears, and that is good. But more likely they will need to *cry out*, expressing their feelings through the strength of action.

Of course, action in the form of over-activity or 'losing oneself in work' may be a means of unrelenting denial – a maladaptive coping response. Even so, such activity can (with prompting) usually be moderated and conscripted into an adaptive process of ritualised action – consciously linking action to emotion/thought/experience.

Men are ingenious in the ritualised action they create for their own healing. For example, a man whose wife died tragically: he remained focussed and protective of his family until the time was right to connect with his grief. He planned and created a large stone wall as a ritual *place* and *activity* in which to allow the full force of his painful emotions and thoughts to emerge. He recounted to a men's group (for men similarly bereaved), how he pushed his pain into each stone block as he heaved it into place. Another example is a man who was exposed to the trauma of a natural disaster: he retrieved an object from the scene and placed it under a rock in a secret location in solitary bushland. He returned to that place, making a ritual journey time and again, uncovering the object and taking it in his hands. In the safety of that place, with that evocative object, he reconnected with, expressed and worked through his experience, until no prompting to return occurred in his thoughts or feelings.[11]

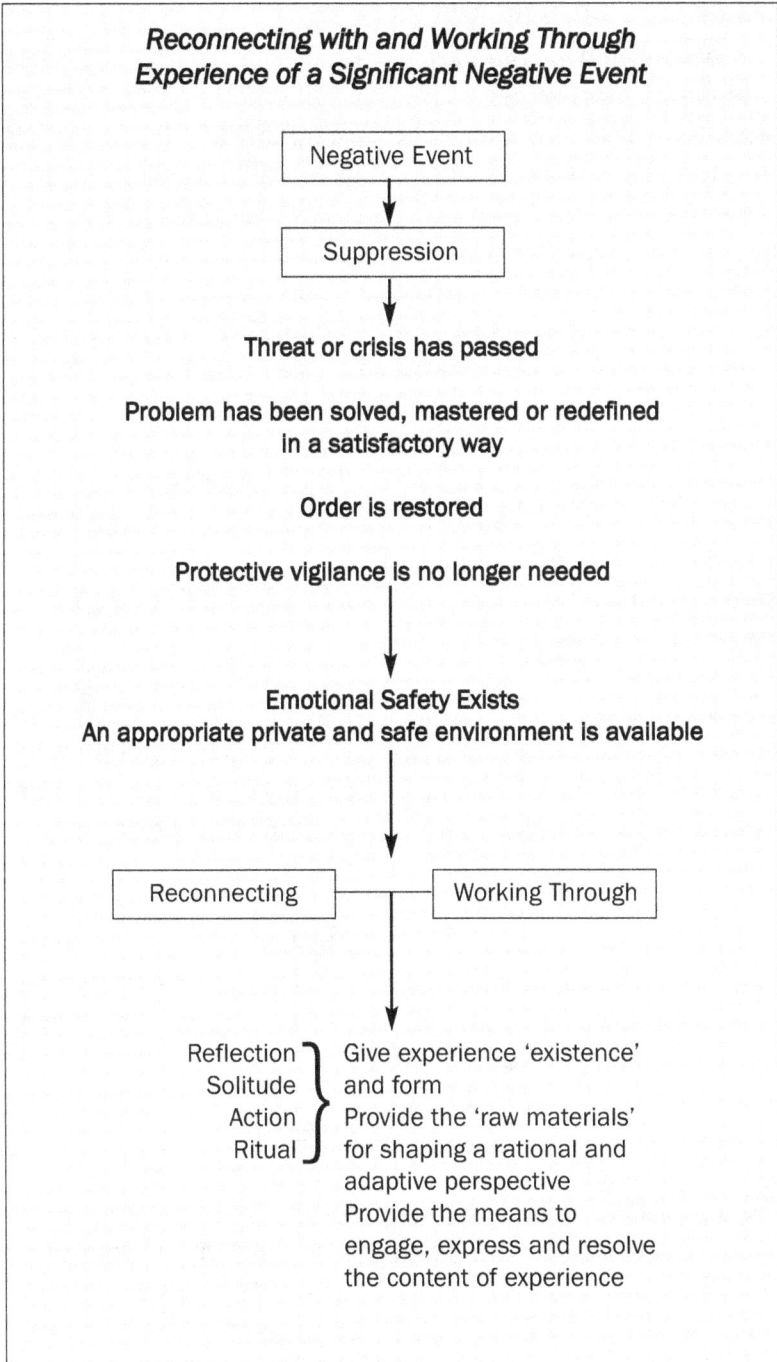

Reconnecting with and Working Through Experience of a Significant Negative Event

Negative Event

↓

Suppression

↓

Threat or crisis has passed

Problem has been solved, mastered or redefined in a satisfactory way

Order is restored

Protective vigilance is no longer needed

↓

Emotional Safety Exists
An appropriate private and safe environment is available

↓

| Reconnecting |—|— Working Through |

↓

Reflection ⎫
Solitude ⎬ Give experience 'existence' and form
Action ⎪ Provide the 'raw materials'
Ritual ⎭ for shaping a rational and adaptive perspective
Provide the means to engage, express and resolve the content of experience

Table 3

DEFINING WHAT IT MEANS TO COPE

Some research on gender differences in coping indicates that males tend to use more adaptive forms of coping than females.[12] The only consistent exception to this pattern is that females are more likely than males to seek help from others, which may be more adaptive.[13] But this is deceptive, because it is vital to understand that coping does not occur in a cultural vacuum – divorced from societal expectations and sex-specific roles. Nor is it separable from male and female biology, which predisposes them to feel, think and behave in particular sex-specific ways. And (as we will see) though it may be true to say that relative to a particular category of experience (or categories of experience) men cope, compared to women, more adaptively; viewed in the broader context of biology and culture, human survival and social adaptiveness, it may be more correct to infer merely *overall comparative difference*.

The phenomenon of coping is actually more complex than popularly thought. And it is not easy to define. The definition proposed here is a basic definition only, but it does include fundamental criteria common within the literature on coping.

Coping may be described as the effective use of any number of behavioural, psychological, internal or external strategies, to achieve psychological stability, to be able to maintain or quickly restore effective functioning in the face of a significantly challenging event, and to minimise the negative impact of such an event.[14/15]

Coping generally involves the use of defensive strategies (like suppression, denial, sublimation), more conscious cognitive strategies (like reframing, reappraising, reconstruing), behavioural strategies (like verbal expressiveness, rapport building, problem solving, ritualised action, rumination), and social support (seeking out and/or accepting assistance from another person or persons).

INDICATORS OF COPING

A popular perception, consistent with the notion that men tend to be less emotionally and psychologically adept than women, is that men have poorer **mental health** compared to women. However, the data simply do not support this perception.

If substance use disorders are included in the catalogue of mental disorders (having more than twice the prevalence amongst men compared to women), men and women in Australia (approximating other Western societies), have similar overall prevalence rates of mental disorder.[16/17] However, from age 35 years, women are more likely to have a mental disorder than men.[18] And, though men are twice as likely than women to have substance abuse disorders, depressed women are more likely than men to develop substance abuse disorders after they become depressed (women are also at greater risk, earlier, of brain and liver damage due to alcoholism).[19/20]

Women are twice as likely to suffer from depression compared to men, and, though men are equally as likely to develop bi-polar affective disorder, women are more likely to be diagnosed with 'rapid cycling' (as many as three episodes in a year).[21]

There are particular issues for women across the reproductive cycle and the menstrual cycle which indicate clearly that 'gender is not a political issue. It is a true biological issue that affects the frequency and expression of mental illness'.[22]

It is well known that certain cognitive styles, such as rumination ('replaying' negative emotional experiences and their possible meanings and consequences) and an exaggerated need for control, increase the risk of depression. This ineffective quest for control, which exacerbates negative thinking, impairs clear thinking and problem solving, and worsens mood state, is more common in women than men.[23] It is also known that women are preferentially affected by life stress, and experience more event associated depression than do men. In approximately 70% of episodes of major depression, a stressful life event is an antecedent, probably acting as a trigger.[24]

Gender differences in mental illness – particularly depression – have often been explained as 'artefacts of society' and the 'gendered landscape' of psychiatric classification and diagnosis.[25] However, as the director of the U.S. National Institute of Mental Health asserts:

> ...research suggests this is not the case. Across many different societies, the rate of schizophrenia and bi-polar disorder are the same. And while depression occurs in different societies at different times, at different rates, the symptoms are always the same and the gender ratio is always two to one (female:male).[26]

Several other diverse and contrasting indices of sex-specific coping effectiveness are also worth mentioning here. For example, a study of bushfire victims 12 months and 20 months after the event, found that **post-traumatic psychiatric morbidity** (depression, somatic complaints and anxiety) was significantly higher in women than men.[27]

A study of sex-specific differences in **acute somatic and psychological reactions to moderate orthopaedic injury**, indicated that women compared with men (both having similar injuries) exhibited significantly greater adverse somatic and psychological reactions.[28]

The experience of **grief resulting from bereavement**, though common, is a potentially highly stressful, disorganising and painful psychological event. Few events rival bereavement in its negative effect; it can unleash a powerful array of emotions and a range of personal, social and practical challenges; it can tax to the limit the coping endurance and capacity of the most resilient person. Taking into consideration sex-specific differences in mental health (irrespective of bereavement effects), grief research suggests that male widowers are relatively more vulnerable to physical and mental health risks than are female widows.[29] However, what may explain this disparity is the degree to which men appear to benefit (more than women) psychologically from being married and that, when widowed, men generally find themselves more socially and emotionally isolated than women – having sometimes dire consequences for their health.[30/31/32/33]

What is particularly illuminating from grief research are the characteristic ways in which widowers, compared with widows, encounter difficulties, and the sex-specific coping orientations they exhibit. A number of studies indicate that when men have difficulty grieving adaptively, they tend to misuse alcohol – much as women do when they encounter difficulties of depressive illness. Though as we have noted, widowers have a relatively greater problem with depression than widows.[34/35]

Men and women who are grieving have been observed to cope in quite different ways. Widows appear to be able to engage and express emotions more easily, and utilise same-sex social support more than widowers. Widowers tend much more to distract themselves, and get on with attending to life changes and the problems concurrent with bereavement.[36] When widows encounter difficulty (as we might expect), though they tend to be confronting of their emotions, they often do so to the neglect of the practical tasks that bereavement brings. Men who encounter difficulties tend to attend well to practical demands, yet to the neglect of working through the emotional component of bereavement. It has been observed that men and women have better grief outcomes when they are able to oscillate between what is termed 'loss and restoration oriented coping'.[37]

Perhaps one of the most publicised and perennial (alleged) 'proofs' of male emotional deficiency, and the male determination to 'oppress and control women', is that of domestic violence. Gender feminism has been keen to highlight examples of male atrocity against women and children as a potent 'fact' of the pathology of masculinity. Successive Australian governments, policy makers, the mass media and even some academics, have happily aligned themselves with this assertion for their own sometimes self-serving reasons. But what is the 'proof'; what are the 'facts'? Are men the uncaring, emotionally underdeveloped, and inherently violent 'control freaks' that many millions of government dollars have been spent to warn us all about?

Quite apart from the relevance these questions have *per se*, they have much importance to our endeavour here of establishing some basis for how well men cope compared with women. Surely an important comparative measure of emotional/psychological coping and competence is **how well men and women handle conflict?** An especially telling sign of not coping with interpersonal conflict, is when women and men resort to violence against each other.

Previously it was noted that research indicates women have been found to express more anger, hostility and negative emotions in intimate relationships than men.[38/39/40] But are men more violent in these relationships than women? Are they less able to cope with interpersonal conflict?

Good Australian data are hard to come by on this issue. Much of what is passed off as 'research' is methodologically flawed 'advocacy research' – 'research' conducted in such a way as to ensure that the kinds of data gathered support the ideological preconceptions of the researchers (a practice apparently condoned – or at least ignored by some government institutions and university faculties). Despite these problems of available local data, more than 125 scholarly investigations (including over 100 empirical studies) across major Western populations, dating from 2001 back to 1975 clearly indicate:

- Women are as physically violent or more violent than men in their relationships; women's violence against men has been shown to have increased, while men's violence towards women has decreased.[41/42/43/44]

- Violence runs in couples. In over 50% of partnerships in which violence was found to occur, both partners struck each other.[45]

- According to assault rates based solely on the responses of women, men are more likely to be assaulted by their female partners.[46]

- Of 41% of injuries sustained due to relationship violence, although more women than men were hurt, the difference was not great with 47% of women compared to 31% of men reporting injury.[47]

- Women are almost as likely to kill as men, in spousal relationships. Of urban spouses convicted of murdering a spouse, 41% are wives.[48]

- Also to be noted is that 58% of homicides committed by women are premeditated; out of every 100 women who kill in domestic situations, 78 have criminal histories, and 55 have a history of violence.[49]

It is quite likely that men experience more violence from female partners than the data reflect, for the obvious reason that men are reluctant to acknowledge that they have been assaulted or abused; to do so would reflect poorly on their identity as men.[50]

What of the claim (and popular slogan): 'Domestic violence is the weapon men use to control women in relationships'? Do struggles for power in intimate relationships arise solely out of men's desire for control?

The reality of relationships is that conflict does and will occur, quite simply because *both* partners struggle with getting their own particular needs met, and to achieve demarcations and control within the relationship which reflect their own individual aspirations, area of interest and expertise. Both partners naturally jostle for the power and control needed to serve their own agendas and to achieve an agreeable compromise essential to a successful relationship. Both engage in power struggles, and, as the data suggest, both have about the same tendency to resort to violence.

If domestic violence is a male prerogative – a weapon men use to control and exploit women, why, one might reasonably ask, has there been found to be a greater degree of violence in lesbian compared with heterosexual relationships?[51] This further underscores the complexity of the whole issue of relationship violence, and the simplistic illegitimacy of the prevailing view.

The most important issue at stake here is not so much that of women's violence comparative to men's violence, but that we don't properly understand the problem of domestic violence, and consequently have yet to formulate an equitable and effective remedy. Unfortunately for females and males that experience or participate in relationship violence, anti-male ideology has consistently undermined and obstructed the intelligent discussion, research and creative work needed to address this issue.

Another example of current ignorance and misconception about domestic violence is the argument of self-defence. Exponents of the politically correct view have asserted that women generally only use violence in self-defence – which explains the 'anomaly' of female to male partner violence. Actually this explains very little. Undoubtedly some women may use violence (as do men) as a means of self-defence, but authoritative data suggest that 'many women's perpetration is motivated by the same interpersonal psychological factors that motivate men's perpetration of violence against their partners'.[52]

Even if self-defence could be used as an explanation of violence towards an intimate partner, this cannot explain why women (in a study of huge scope) who had hit their partners were '4.4 times as likely to have committed a violent crime against someone other than an intimate partner'.[53] More telling still is the evidence indicating that one fifth of all violent offenders in the U.S. are women, and their victims are mostly other women – 75% in fact.[54] This surely suggests that some women's capacity for violence extends beyond what can be explained in terms of self-defence occasioned by male violence. The authors of a recent longitudinal study who have explored this idea of self-defence with considerable thoroughness, conclude that:

> *The sex similarity on partner violence appears to be robust, applies to clinically significant couples whose abuse is injurious, treated and/or adjudicated, and cannot be explained by the hypothesis that women's aggression is self-defence.*[55]

One final example of how current popular assumptions about men's violence and women's self-defence do not stack up is in relation to child abuse. Though men are chiefly responsible for the sexual maltreatment of children, most physical abuse of children is not perpetrated by men but by women; with the single largest group of abusers being mothers.[56] In a major national U.S. report, it was noted that, where maltreatment resulted in the death of a child, 78% of perpetrators were female, and the abuse of boys was four times higher than that of girls.[57]

What we observe of men and women in conflict, though in many ways appearing anomalous (and all the more so due to dominant ideological assumptions on the matter), may be partly explained by our cultural emphasis on the privacy of intimate and domestic relations. It seems that both women and men are less inclined to conform with their usual role demands and obligations, 'behind closed doors'. On balance, it appears no less contrary to biological and cultural imperatives that either women or men should choose to engage in partner/domestic violence.

Something that should also not be overlooked here is the measure of male restraint in partner/domestic relations, attributable to the masculine (and manhood) imperative of protectiveness. It is an irony that the cultural taboo which prohibits men from hurting women, exploited by gender feminist propagandism to influence societal opinion against men, depends for its robustness on the core masculine biological and cultural imperative to protect women – the imperative that the same feminists have impugned as sexist and oppressive.

It may be argued that by putting masculinity in the frame as the 'root cause and reason for domestic violence', gender feminists miss the point that the degree to which men are responsible for such violence is more likely because of *too little* rather than too much masculine influence. Certainly a case can be made (as will occur later) that males need more balanced and 'well rounded' behavioural and role socialisation; and doubtless the world would be a better place if more males were properly supported in attaining a viable and mature masculine gender identity. But what has tended to happen in the irrationality of ideological fervour is that the proverbial baby has been thrown out with the bathwater.

If resort to violence in intimate relationships is an obvious and/or significant sign of not handling conflict – not coping effectively, it is reasonable to infer that men on average appear to cope no less poorly than women. This inference of course suggests that not only is there a serious problem with current assumptions about relationship violence (and the whole edifice of programs, literature and policy based on them), but as well a serious injustice against men. There should be no argument that relationship violence is a problem which we must attempt to remedy, but women *and* men must accept responsibility for doing so.

SOCIAL SUPPORT

An important dimension of coping – especially in relation to men, is social support. Whilst it is well recognised that men suffer needlessly for want of the support of others at times of personal difficulty, much ignorance exists about why it is that men need a quite different context of social support compared with women, one which is not often available to them.

There is considerable evidence that social support involving social ties plays a major role in cushioning the psychological impact of potentially harmful events. Emotional support – as well as the perceived availability of support, are both likely to buffer the deleterious effects of stress on health and to be protective of mental health.[58]   Research also indicates that social support may even influence mortality, through changes in cardiovascular, endocrine, and immune systems.[59]

The ways in which social ties might provide this support may include tangible help – like with money, practical assistance, information, advice – or emotional support, which may include another person (or persons) being genuinely concerned, available to listen, or prepared to be patiently 'present'.[60] But it is also thought that social support can consist of anything that gives rise to a person perceiving himself or herself as the 'recipient of positive affect...or believing that they are cared for, loved and valued'.[61]

DO MEN AND WOMEN BENEFIT EQUALLY FROM SOCIAL SUPPORT?

The limited research available on this question suggests that women gain most benefit from social support[62] – which appears consistent with the on-average female orientation (favouring rapport building and verbal intimacy and expressiveness), and current opportunities within our culture for female social support. But more research is needed, both to examine more closely the types and sources of social support men most benefit from, and in what ways ideologically driven cultural changes (in recent decades) have diminished opportunities of acceptable and appropriate social support for men.

There is little doubt, based on even a cursory glance at literature of the dominant men's movement in the U.S. (the post-feminist mythopoetic movement), that men report not only benefiting from social support, but benefiting most and in particular ways from the support afforded by other men.[63] Why this is so is unfortunately not often realised or understood by health and welfare professionals, women or even men themselves.

The Importance of Men Supporting Other Men

Previously noted was that:

> *Female conversation and group behaviour centre around feelings, inclusion, relatedness, connectedness and relationships, with a propensity for self-disclosure and the verbal expression of emotions. "Women feel close to other women when talking face-to-face".[64]*

In contrast to this orientation, we observed that male conversation and group behaviour centre around activities, and that men favour communication that preserves their independence and autonomy; also, that male communication tends to be abstract, metaphorical, constructive, candid, confronting and confrontingly humorous.[65]

Men tend to feel close to each other on the occasion of working or playing side-by-side, engaged in activities. Women express intimacy and support each other by doing things for and with each other, but more for the opportunity of verbal intimacy.[66]

> *Even when men comfort each other in crisis situations…it is physical presence rather than intimate talk that tends to be most valued.[67]*

There is a fascinating history associated with the role of male-only groups and societies. The current activities of men's groups, mainly in North America (though also in Britain and Australia), emanating from the Mythopoetic Men's Movement, are in some elements strongly reminiscent of the past.[68] With an emphasis on ritual, ceremony, and the great value of safe male 'ritual space' (highly important in past fraternal organisations), and with various borrowings from North American Indian rituals and spirituality (to name but one source), these groups have sometimes been summarily dismissed (particularly by profeminists) as mere novelties of an oppressive masculinity, worthy only of condemnation. However, to date there has been no serious analytical examination of these groups by their critics – including those who claim to have done so.[69]

Whilst it may be the case that some of the rhetoric and practices of some of these groups appear and may be plainly silly,* such groups nevertheless present some profound and important insights into how men can benefit from each others' support, and from nurturing each others' psychological well being.

The safe male 'ritual space' these groups appear to provide is made possible because of an agreed suspension of usual competitiveness, and out of a reasoned and compassionate endeavour to be mutually supportive in a uniquely male way; thus allowing men to discuss their thoughts and exhibit vulnerability, with understanding and each others' strict confidentiality.[70]

Historically, the secrecy and exclusivity of some men's groups has been often misunderstood (what people don't understand they tend to fear), and yet these features (in most examples) simply indicate men's need of each others' company and support, and their need of assured 'safety' before displaying their vulnerability in much needed ritualised action. Men's general aversion to public emotionality, and that male ritual practices of their very nature (because they permit honesty, self-disclosure forms of emotional expressivity and vulnerability) require strict privacy and to be away from and distinct from female

---

* Some native American based men's work directly expropriates cultural materials without contextual adaptation, rendering them as a form of exotic ritual drama without connection to the lives of people.

activities, simply reflects that men and women have some uniquely different needs that can only be met in the same-sex 'society of others'.

Just as men and women are brought up and must function in largely different cultural domains, and linguistically construct reality and their place in the world in sex-specific ways, the contexts in which they experience meaningful social support will also be significantly dissimilar.[71/72]

It is not only from conspicuously ritual-oriented groups that men derive benefit. In all-male groups set up for mutual support and therapy men have been found to easily suspend their usual competitiveness and status maintenance behaviours. In groups of this kind men are characteristically courageous and highly supportive of each other. They tend not to entertain disruptive hidden agendas, quickly develop emotional bonds, and appear genuinely egalitarian.[73]

In a report on men's counselling research submitted to the Australian Commonwealth Government's Attorney General's Department (Family Services Branch), special comment was made on how striking and surprising it was to observe the willingness of men in all-male groups to talk about personal relationship issues. The authors noted that:

> ...this was true across older and younger groups, across blue collar and white collar males, and in city and regional locations.[74]

The authors of this report further commented:

> This is a particularly notable result in that it goes counter to the beliefs of many women.[75]

Men's health researchers also concur with the positive potential of all-male groups, suggesting that in such groups an appreciable positive change in men's amenability to self-care messages about health can occur. Men have shown a preparedness in this setting to change their health behaviour (usually otherwise resistant to change) if to do so is an agreed male group behaviour.[76] There is ample evidence that men can benefit significantly and in a range of ways from men's groups and male-only gatherings. And, as will be discussed later, such contexts are essential to ensuring adequate opportunities for healthy male development, the principal feature of which will be making a successful transition from immature 'boy psychology' to mature 'man psychology'.[77]

Male-only environments have been under siege for decades. Much legal and social pressure has been brought to bear on demanding that women should be able to gain admission to clubs, groups and organisations that formerly excluded females, completely ignorant of the significant and important role they performed. This pressure is perhaps only less common in recent times because most male-only groups have been broken down. Men have been left with very few male-only environments. The disquieting emphasis in all of this is the undeniable message that:

> *...men must be like women and women can be whatever they like.*[78]

Why has gender feminism been so critical of male-only groups and so determined to break them down? Quite simply because feminist social constructionism declares that male-only groups only serve to perpetuate the oppressive 'masculine principle'; they encourage a 'flight from femininity' contrary to the need for men to be demasculinised and feminised; they discourage genuine self-development because they do not have as their central activity a process of awareness raising, concerning the oppressiveness of masculinity and patriarchy; they also serve to validate and reinforce masculine self-identity and the narratives by which men continue to oppress and control women.[79]

Interestingly, even male groups set up by the early men's liberation movement, expressly to deconstruct masculinity and feminise men in compliance with gender feminist dogma, were disdained and held in contempt. Gender feminists declared that, 'men in groups are men in bad company', and that anti-sexist men 'were worse than the old breed'; despite these men trying to change themselves as entirely as they could to suit what they believed feminists desired (a salutary caution for male profeminist enthusiasts!)[80/81]

No-one could argue that there are not some all-male groups, activities and environments that tend to foster inappropriate attitudes towards women and immature juvenile male behaviour. But this is no more true in general than it is of all-female groups, activities and environments fostering inappropriate attitudes towards men and immature juvenile behaviour. And certainly in the realm of gender politics, gender feminism has an unsurpassed reputation for its demeaning and vitriolic rhetoric targeting men.[82] It is fair to say that much work lies ahead for women and men in getting their 'own houses in order' when it comes to appropriate behaviour and gender equity.

Based on the data and observations we have considered concerning *Men and Coping*, it is possible to make a number of inferences. When viewed in the proper context of biology (and biological imperatives) and culture (expressed through normative role demands), how women and men cope and the strategies they employ overall cannot be described (expect in particular instances and examples) as more or less competent; they are better described as *significantly different*. For example, women ruminate and are verbally emotionally expressive; but that is consistent with their sex-specific biology, cultural conditioning, and the kind of roles they perform. Men suppress, are less concerned with relationships, and are generally verbal and emotional economists; but that is likewise consistent with their sex-specific biology, cultural conditioning, and the roles they must perform.

We need to be very clear on this point: women and men are different, they conduct their emotional lives differently (on average), they favour different cognitive and coping styles and orientations, and they linguistically construct reality in different ways with different outcomes. Difference here does not mean deficiency; rather it reflects necessity and, difficult or not, much needed complementarity. Nor is difference the same as preference: some women may prefer men to be more verbally and emotionally expressive and less action oriented; some men may prefer women to be less emotional and more practical – and there is room for negotiation here. But we achieve nothing by pretending that difference is only a preference, or that it does not or should not exist.

When we are all done with the threadbare nonsense of a genderless or femocentric utopia, or that difference can simply be erased by a whim of idcological prejudice, perhaps we will be able to apply ourselves to understanding and working with our differences; perhaps we will be able to work out more complementary constructions of gender and behaviour, that reconcile rather than polarise, and that aim for gender equity rather than comparative advantage. For when all is said and done:

> *Cooperation between men and women has always been critical to human survival, and the realities of men and women have always been complementary aspects of the total reality that is our symbolic universe.*[83]

However fanciful our ideological aspirations, survival is the primary imperative of evolutionary history.

Our differences have been the basis of our survival and, however problematic they may be to our preferences, they are deserving of a good deal more respect and understanding than they have been given.

In the next chapter we will examine in detail the characteristic differences between men's and women's styles of communication and, again, why it is so important to understand these differences in the light of both biological and cultural realities. As will be argued, such an understanding is very important for avoiding unnecessary misunderstandings of communication, and for promoting satisfying and functional interpersonal relationships.

References

1. Nolan, P., **Defences, Resources** (online, 1999) Available online – http://www.psychpage.com

2. Stout, J., **Repression And Suppression** (online, date unknown) Available online – http://stout.bravepages.com/h/repress.htm

3. Sawrikar, P. and Hunt, C. J., **The Relationship Between Suppressing Negative Emotions and Mental Health Among Adolescents**. *Cognition and Emotion (in review)* 2003

4. Ibid.

5. Ibid.

6. Ibid.

7. Gist, R., Lubin, B., Redburn, B., **Psychosocial, Ecological, and Community Perspectives on Disaster Response** *Loss*, 1998, pp. 3, 25-51

8. Charlton, P. and Thomson, J., **Ways of Coping With Psychological Distress After Trauma** *British Journal of Clinical Psychology*, 1996, pp. 35, 517-530

9. Golden, T., **Different Paths Toward Healing: The Experience and Healing of a Man's Grief** (10400 Connecticut Ave. Suite 514, Kensington, Maryland, 20595, 1994)

10. Ibid.

11. Author's recollections of men's stories from a therapy group run for bereaved men (Adelaide, 1995)

12. Weiden, G. and Collins, R., **Gender Coping and Health** in Krohn. E. (ed.) **Attention and Avoidance: Strategies**

in Coping With Aversiveness (Seattle, WA, Aogrefe and Huber, 1993)

13. Miller, S. and Kirsch, N., **Sex Differences In Cognitive Coping With Stress** *in* Barrett, R., Biener, L., Barnch, G., (eds.), **Gender and Stress** (New York, Free Press, 1987) pp. 278-307

14. Newton, J., **Preventing Mental Illness** (London, Routledge, 1993) pp. 142-164

15. Holger, V., Eivind, B., Seymour, L., (eds.), **Psychobiology of Stress: A Study of Coping Men** (London, Academic Press, 1978)

16. **Mental Health and Wellbeing: Profile of Adults, Australia** (Canberra, Australian Bureau of Statistics, 1997)

17. Andres, G., Hall, W., Teesson, M., Henderson, S., **The Mental Health of Australia** (Canberra, ACT, Commonwealth Department of Health and Family Services, Mental Health Branch, 1999)

18. Op. cit., Mental Health and Wellbeing: Profile of adults, Australia, 1997

19. Ibid.

20. **National Institute of Mental Health, Conference Summary of Gender Differences In Depression** (U.S.A. 2001) Available online –
http://www.nimh.nih.gov

21. Ibid.

22. Ibid.

23. Ibid.

24. Ibid.

25. Bufield, J., **The Archaeology Of Psychiatric Disorder: Gender and Disorders of Thought, Emotion and**

Behaviour *in* Bendelow, G., Carpenter, M., Vantier, C., Williams, S., **Gender Health and Healing: The Public/Private Divide** (London, Routledge, 2002)

26. Op. cit., National Institute of Mental Health, 2001.

27. McFarlane, A., Clayer, J., Bookless, C., **Psychiatric Morbidity Following A Natural Disaster: An Australian Bushfire** (Australia, University of Adelaide Department of Psychiatry, Queen Elizabeth Hospital, 1996)

28. Ponzar, S., Johansson, L., Johansson, S., **Gender Differences in Acute Somatic and Psychological Reactions to Moderate Orthopaedic Injuries** *European Journal of Trauma*, 2001, Vol. 27, Issue 1

29. Stroebe, M., **New Directions in Bereavement Research: Exploration of Gender Differences** *Palliative Medicine*, 1998, 12, pp. 5-12

30. Umberson, D., Wortman, C., Kessler, R., **Widowhood and Depression: Explaining Long-term Gender Differences In Vulnerability**. *Journal of Health and Social Behaviour*, 1992, 33, pp. 10-24

31. Belle, D., **Gender Differences In The Social Moderation of Stress** *in* Barnett, R., Bieher, L., Baruch, G. (eds.), **Gender And Stress** (New York, The Free Press, 1987) pp. 257-277

32. Ferraro, K., Mutran, E., Barresi, C., **Widowhood Health and Friendship In Later Life** *Journal of Health and Social Behaviour*, 1984, 25, pp. 245-259

33. Lazarus, R. and Folkman, S., **Stress Appraisal and Coping** (New York, Springer, 1984)

34. Cramer, D., **Living Alone, Marital Status, Gender and Health** *Journal of Applied Community Social Psychology*, 1993, 3, pp. 1-15

35. Joung, I., Van der Meer, J., Machenbach, J., **Marital**

Status and Health Care Utilisation *International Journal of Epidemiology*, 1995, 24, pp. 569-575

36. Op. cit., Stroebe, 1998

37. Ibid.

38. Dosser, D., Balswich, J., Halveston, D., **Situational Content of Emotional Expressions** *Journal of Counselling Psychology*, 1983, 31, pp. 375-384

39. Kelly, H., Cunningham, J., Grisham, J,, Lefebvre, L., Sink, C., Yablon, G., **Sex Differences Made During Conflict Within Heterosexual Pairs** *Sex Roles*, 1978, pp. 4, 473-492

40. Shimanoff, S., **The Role of Gender In Linguistic References To Emotive Status** *Communication Quarterly*, 1983, 31, pp. 174-179

41. Fiebert, M., **References Examining Assault By Women On Their Spouses or Male Partners** (California State University, 2001) Available online – www.menweb.org/fiebert.htm

42. Strauss, M. and Gelles, R., **Societal Change and Change In Family Violence From 1975-1985 As Revealed by Two National Surveys** *Journal of Marriage And the Family*, 1986, 48, pp. 465-479

43. Sugarman, D. and Notaling, G., **Dating Violence: Prevalence Context And Risk Markers** *in* Pirog-Good, M. and Stets, J., (eds.). **Violence in Dating Relationships: Emerging Social Issues** (New York, Praeger, 1989)

44. Walker, L., **The Battered Women Syndrome** (New York, Springer Publishing Company, 1984)

45. Headey, B., Scott, D., DeVaus, D., **Domestic Violence In Australia: Are Women and Men Equally Violent?** University of Melbourne, La Trobe University (date

unknown) Available online, posted Feb 2004 –http://www.mensrights.com.au

46. Op. cit., Strauss & Gelles, 1986

47. **Domestic Violence, Findings From the British Crime Survey** (U.K. Home Office Research, Development and Statistics Directorate, 1996)

48. **Bureau of Justice Statistics, Murder in families** (U.S. Department of Justice, July, 1994)

49. Mann, C., **Getting Even? Women Who Kill in Domestic Encounters** *Justice Quarterly*, 1988, No. 1

50. Steinmetz, S. and Lucca, J., **Husband Battering** *in* Can Hasselt, V. et al. (eds.), **Handbook of Family Violence** (New York, Plenium Press, 1988)

51. Garcia, J., **The Cost Of Escaping Domestic Violence** *Los Angeles Times*, May 5th 1991

52. Moffit, T., Caspi, A., Rutter, M., Silva, P., **Differences In Antisocial Behaviour: Conduct Disorder, Delinquency, And Violence In The Dunedin Longitudinal Study** (Cambridge, Cambridge University Press, 2001)

53. Ibid.

54. Greenfield, L. and Sneel, T., **Women Offenders, Bureau Of Justice Statistics Special Report** NCJ175688 (Washington D.C. Department of Justice, 1999)

55. Op. cit., Moffit et al., 2001

56. Tomison, A., **Protecting Children: Updating the National Picture** *in* **Child Welfare Services** series no. 16 (Canberra, AGPS, 1996)

57. **United States National Incidence of Child Abuse and Neglect Report, 1995**

58. Kessler, R. and McLeod, J., **Social Support And Psychological Distress In Community Surveys** *in*

Cohen, S., and Sym, L., (eds.), **Social Support and Health** (New York, Academic Press, 1984)

59. Uchnio, B., Cacioppo, J., Kiecolt-Glasser, K., **The Relationships Between Social Support And Physiological Processes: A Review With Emphasis on Underlying Mechanisms and Implications for Health** *Physiological Bulletin*, 1996, pp. 119, 488-531

60. Op. cit., Newton, 1993

61. Cobb, S., **Social Support As A Moderator Of Life Stress** *Psychosomatic Medicine*, 1976, 38, pp. 300-314

62. Perrewé, P. and Carlson, D., **Do Men and Women Benefit From Social Support Equally? Results From A Field Examination Within The Work And Family Context** *in* Nelson, D. and Burke, R., **Gender Workstress and Health** (USA, American Psychological Association, 2002)

63. Harding, C., (ed.) **Wingspan: Inside The Men's Movement** (New York, St. Martin's Press, 1992)

64. Ashfield, J., **Gender, Masculinity and Manhood: Core Concepts for Understanding Men's Issues** (Western Australia, Ikon Publications, 2003), p115. *This Book has been revised and reissued under the title: The Making Of A Man: Reclaiming masculinity and manhood in the light of reason (South Australia, Peacock Publications, 2004)*

65. Ibid.

66. Ibid.

67. Nadeau, R., **S/He Brain: Science Sexual Politics and the Myths of Feminism** (USA, Praeger, 1996) p. 87

68. Harding, C., **Men's Secret Societies 1890s to 1990s** *in* Harding, C., (ed.) **Wingspan: Inside the Men's Movement**, (New York, Saint Martins Press, 1992)

69. Kimmel, M., **The Politics Of Manhood** (USA Temple University Press, 1995). **Kimmel is perhaps the best known spokesperson of the profeminist movement, a movement renowned for its pseudointellectual criticism of the mythopoetic movement, and its ardent adherence to social constructionist dogma.*

70. Op. cit., Harding, Wingspan, 1992

71. Ibid.

72. Op. cit., Nadeau, 1996, p. 92

73. The author's own clinical experience facilitating men-only groups for The Sudden Infant Death Syndrome Association, Payneham, Adelaide, South Australia, and the Regional Health Services Program, Centre for Rural Men, Melrose, Southern Flinders Ranges

74. Francas, M., Vlais, R., Zapelli, R., **Men's Counselling Research : report to The Attorney General's Department, Family Services Branch**, (Australia, Donavan Research: Marketing and Communications Research Consultants, 1998) p. 5

75. Ibid.

76. Rees, C., Jones, M., Scott, T., **Exploring Men's Health In A Men Only Group** *Nursing Standard*, 1995, 9, 45 p. 38-40

77. Moore, R. and Gillette, D., **King, Warrior, Magician, Lover** (San Francisco, Harper, 1990)

78. Paglia, C., **Sexual Personae: Art And Decadence From Nefertiti To Emily Dickinson** (New York, Vintage Books, 1990) pp. 21 & 22

79. Op. cit., Kimmel, 1995

80. Segal, L., **Slow Motion: Changing Masculinities Changing Men** (London, Virgo Press, 1990) p. 281

81. Ibid., p. 292

82. Sommers, C., **Who Stole Feminism?: How Women Have Betrayed Women** (New York, Simon and Schuster, 1994)

83. Op. cit., Nadeau, p. 138

3

Men and Communication

A perennial problem between men and women is that their biological (and cultural) agendas are in many ways at odds with one another. Though this has certainly served well the evolutionary agenda of survival, it has made the whole business of relationships – particularly with modern expectations of relationships – fraught with irritating incompatibilities and dissatisfaction.

Without doubt, the most publicised dissatisfaction in relationships is that many women find men's communication inadequate. Of course some men do need to work at improving their communication in order to nurture more effective relationships and strengthen affectionate bonds with their female partners. However, it is vitally important that men *and* women acknowledge, understand, and value their sex-specific differences, tempering their expectations accordingly, and negotiating some necessary compromises and 'give and take'.

One of the main reasons cited by women for seeking marital divorce is their dissatisfaction with their husband's interpersonal communication – including the unpreparedness of husbands to verbalise and share their feelings. That might appear straightforward enough, yet research indicates that women view men who exhibit a more feminine orientation in emotionality and self-disclosure as 'too feminine' and 'poorly adjusted'.[1]

Ignoring or misunderstanding the complexities of these phenomena, social constructionists simply assert that men and their behaviour are the problem, and that women are the model both for healthy communication and normalcy in love relationships and marriage. Quite obviously, such an assertion has the potential to contaminate and skew the way many health and human service practitioners perceive the dynamics of problematic relationships – favouring the assumption that any problem is more likely to emanate from the male partner and, therefore, any remedy must in some way aim to demasculinise and feminise him.

Though there may be no simple solution to the dissatisfactions partners experience in interpersonal communication, it can be said with certainty that elevating one gender's preferences over the other's only makes matters worse. What also needs to be stated is that men have their difficulties with women's communication, and they have no less valid reasons for their characteristic ways of communicating than do women. Which brings us back to the different verbal and linguistic styles and capacities of men and women, and their generally different action versus relationship orientations.[2]

One of the most useful and insightful commentaries on this subject is linguist Dehorah Tannen's book *You Just Don't Understand: Women and Men in Conversation*.[3] Tannen observes that there are significant differences in men's and women's use of language and style of communication, with men using conversation 'to preserve their independence and negotiate and maintain status in a hierarchical social order', and women using conversation as 'a way of establishing connections and negotiating relationships'.[4] She suggests that men are more at home with 'report-talk' and they tend to use language that is characterised by assertion and abstraction – they communicate in 'messages'. Their language also tends to be categorical and commanding. Conversely, women tend to be more at home with private conversation or 'rapport talk' – favouring language that employs subtle nuances, covert meanings – communicating in 'metamessages'. And rather than using language that is categorical or commanding, female language is more aimed at achieving consensus and more likely to favour 'conditional propositions'.

Men and women also tend to talk about their status differently: males using a simple profile including individual skills and achievements, and females using elaborate descriptions of overall character. And, whilst men approach problems with suggestions and concrete solutions, women tend to do so with empathy and an emphasis on relationship. Tannen offers useful examples of some of these tendencies of male and female language and communication. She points out that:

> *If women are often frustrated because men do not respond to their troubles by offering matching troubles, men are often frustrated because women do. Some men not only take no comfort in such a response, they take offence.*[5]

She gives an example of a conversation which, as a result of miscommunication, ended in argument.

He: I'm really tired. I didn't sleep well last night.
She: I didn't sleep well either. I never do.
He: Why are you trying to belittle me?
She: I'm not. I'm just trying to show you I understand![6]

Tannen explains:

> This woman was not only hurt by her husband's reaction; she was mystified by it. How could he think she was belittling him? By "belittle", he meant "belittle my experience". He was filtering her attempts to establish connection through his concern with preserving independence and avoiding being put down.[7]

Highlighting the difficulties that can occur between men and women when they express troubles or problems, Tannen observes that women may resent men's tendency to suggest solutions to some problems, whereas men may be irritated by 'women's refusal to take action to solve the problems they complain about'.[8] For many men a woman's complaint or verbalised problem invites a male problem solving response; it is a challenge to their ability to think of and apply a solution. However, though many women may appreciate help with a mechanical or practical problem, 'few are inclined to appreciate help in *fixing* emotional troubles'. She suggests that this explains:

> ...why men are frustrated when their sincere attempts to help a women solve her problems are met not with gratitude but disapproval.[9]

To many men, women seem sometimes to be content just languishing or 'wallowing' in their troubles, wanting to talk about them forever, instead of constructively dealing with them or just laughing them off. This highlights the distinction between 'message' and 'metamessage':

> Trying to solve a problem or fix a trouble focuses on the message level of talk. But for most women who habitually report problems at work or in friendships, the message is not the main point of complaining. It's the metamessage that counts: telling about a problem is a bid for an expression of understanding ("I know how you feel") or a similar complaint ("I felt

the same way when something similar happened to me"). In other words, troubles talk is intended to reinforce rapport by sending the metamessage "we're the same; you're not alone". Women are frustrated when they not only don't get this reinforcement but, quite the opposite, feel distanced by the advice, which seems to send the metamessage "we're not the same". You have the problems; I have the solutions.[10]

The differences in male and female communication that Tannen so insightfully describes reflect with a good deal of accuracy what is now known about the processes of the sex-specific male and female brains. Men using conversation to 'preserve their independence', and women using conversation to establish connections and negotiate relationships reflects accurately 'the conditions of survival for single-sex groups of hunter-gatherers'.[11] These conditions occasioned the 'evolution of sex-differences in brain regions associated with sensory and motor skills'.[12] The connection between the brain regions associated with these skills and the language and conversations favoured by men and women may be explained by, and is likely because:

The development of the more recently evolved brain regions associated with language skills was in concert with and conditioned by previously evolved brain regions associated with the sex-specific sensory and motor skills. This contributed to sex-specific differences in linguistic and other cognitive functions in the neocortex.[13]

It is well known that the male brain hemispheres function in a less collaborative way than is observable in females. Male linguistic constructions of reality are more specific to the left hemisphere and with fewer inputs from the right hemisphere. Male linguistic constructions are consequently more likely to be characterised and constrained by 'lineal, categorical and causal cognitive processes of the left hemisphere'.[14] A limited contribution from the right hemisphere explains why such constructions appear to exhibit 'less awareness of coded meaning in spatial relationships, emotional nuances in behaviour, and vocal intonations that alter the literal meaning of words'.[15] When a problem or task activates right hemispheric specialisations, the solutions the brain constructs will be largely characterised by the more abstract and spatial cognitive process of the right hemisphere. Correspondingly, when such solutions are:

> *...translated into linguistic representations in the left hemisphere, there should be a higher probability that it will reflect the terms of constructing reality associated with the right hemisphere.*[16]

Tannen's ideas about male language tending to be categorical, abstract, 'report-talk,' and communicating 'messages', appear to fit with what is now understood about male brain processes.

The female brain, which incorporates a greater interactive symmetry of left and right hemispheres, permits linguistic constructions of reality which invoke a broader range of right hemispheric functions. This may:

> *...enhance awareness of emotionally relevant details, visual clues, verbal nuances, and hidden meanings. This awareness could also be enhanced by more extensive connectivity to neural patterns that represent associations and memories.*[17]

That the female brain has the capacity to construct linguistic reality out of such a broad range of data, and in relation to 'more extensive and interrelated cognitive and emotional contexts,' indicates not only why women use language that tends to be consensual and that features identification with others, but as well inclines them 'to perceive people and events in a complex web of relation'.[18] Tannen's female 'rapport-talk' and 'metamessages' also appear to find a basis of validation in science.

Other contrasts in men's and women's conversational styles may also be attributable to sex-specific differences in sensory capacity and characteristics. Women, with a range of superior sensitivities (taste, touch, smell, peripheral vision), 'probably factor more refined sensory information into their linguistic constructions'.[19] Whereas male superiority in visual acuity and specificity of sight in the middle of the visual field likely inclines men to:

> *...perceive reality in terms of individual objects. The male's tendency to construct reality in terms of vectors marking distance and direction in map space could be another reason why the language of men tends to be more abstract and object oriented.*[20]

As already noted, much evidence indicates that female conversation and group behaviour centre around feelings, inclusion, relatedness, connectedness and relationships, with a propensity for self-disclosure and the verbal expression of emotions.[21] In contrast, male conversation and group behaviour tends to centre around action and activities. Men are usually careful to measure self-disclosure and ensure personal space that allows for the preservation of autonomy. They favour constructive, candid verbal communication – and the use of uniquely male non-verbal communication.

It is plainly evident from these brief observations that there is much more to the whole issue of men's and women's communication 'than meets the eye'. What has been shown here should caution men and women (irrespective of ideological persuasion) against simplistic accusations of deficiency in communication, and instead provide a basis for taking account of difference in order to reasonably negotiate preference.

Thus far we have examined some of the significant differences in the way men and women conduct their emotional lives, cope with negative life events, tend to linguistically construct reality, and communicate. But it is also vital that we understand just how different are the processes and expectations involved in how males and females attain to a sense of individual autonomous adulthood and meaningful gender identity. As we will see in the following chapter, for boys this poses special demands, difficulties, and potential problems. This understanding is indispensable to even the most basic grasp of masculine psychology and gender issues.

Comparative (on average) Male/Female Sex-specific Communication Styles

MALES	FEMALES
Tend to use conversation to preserve their independence and negotiate and maintain their status in a hierarchical social order.	Use conversation to establish connections and negotiate relationships.
Are more at home with 'report talk' which employs language that is assertive and abstract; they communicate in 'messages'.	Are more at home with 'rapport talk' which employs language that has subtle nuances and covert meanings; they communicate in 'metamessages'.
Tend to use language that is direct, categorical and commanding.	Tend to use language aimed at achieving consensus, and of a kind that suggests 'conditional propositions'.
Approach problems with suggestions and concrete solutions.	Tend to approach problems with a concern for empathy and relationship.
May be irritated by women's refusal to take action to solve problems complained about.	May resent men's tendency to suggest solutions to some problems.
Often perceive a woman's complaint or verbalised problem as inviting a male problem solving response, and as a challenge to think of and apply a solution.	May appreciate help with a mechanical or practical problem, but may not appreciate help with *fixing* emotional troubles.
Conversation and group behaviour tend to centre around action and activities.	Telling about a problem is often a bid for an expression of understanding; 'trouble talk' is intended to reinforce rapport.
Carefully measure self-disclosure, seek to preserve autonomy, and favour constructive, candid and economical communication.	Conversation and group behaviour centre around feelings, inclusion and relationship.
	Favour self-disclosure (of a kind that is relatively uninhibited), and the verbal and outward expression of emotions.

Table 4

References

1. Nadeau, R., **S/He Brain**: **Science, Sexual Politics And The Myths Of Feminism** (U.S.A., Praeger, 1996) p. 94

2. Ashfield, J., **Gender, Masculinity and Manhood: Core Concepts for Understanding Men's Issues** (Western Australia, Ikon Publications, 2003) p. 115. *This Book has been revised and reissued under the title:* **The Making Of A Man: Reclaiming masculinity and manhood in the light of reason** *(South Australia, Peacock Publications, 2004)*

3. Tannen, D., **You Just Don't Understand: Women and Men In Conversation** (New York, Ballantine Books, 1990)

3. Ibid., p. 77

4. Ibid., p. 51

5. Ibid.

6. Ibid.

7. Ibid., p. 52

8. Ibid.

9. Ibid., p. 53

10. Op. cit., Nadeau, p. 84

11. Ibid.

12. Ibid.

13. Ibid., pp. 84 & 85

14. Ibid., p. 85

15. Ibid.

16.   Ibid., p. 86

17.   Ibid.

18.   Ibid.

19.   Ibid., pp. 86 & 87

20.   Ibid., p. 87

4

Men and Manhood

A whole new literature is now emerging focussing on the problems of becoming and being a man in today's world. Sadly though, even the sophisticated 'textbook' renditions of this theme can't seem to break away from or think outside the feminist social constructionist 'square'.[1] They appear to intelligently identify many issues worthy of consideration but are forced to engage in overly laboured and elaborated analyses (resulting in paradigms that are conspicuously subjective), because of the limited knowledge and data allowable within the ideological framework to which they subscribe. This is a lamentable loss of intellectual expenditure which could be so much better utilised to tackle this important theme.

The topics of male development, male socialisation and manhood are key elements in understanding male gender psychology. Making clear sense of what these elements entail provides insight into how inherently difficult, potentially traumatic and problematic the whole business of growing up as a male, and becoming and being recognised as a man can be.

To commence our examination of these elements it is important here to reiterate the definitions of masculinity and manhood previously presented.

Masculinity refers to male specific 'biologically innate cognitive and emotional processes and capacities, and the male-specific abilities and behaviours they give rise to'.[2] When these male-specific abilities and behaviours are adapted to, shaped by, and made specific to a particular cultural and environmental setting by social learning and cultural conditioning, the effect or result (in adult males) is best described as *manhood.* Manhood in any particular culture exhibits what is generally considered to be manly or manliness.[3]

THE NEEDS OF SOCIETY AND THE MANHOOD IDEAL

A question of immense contemporary importance is: Why is it so hard for boys to achieve some sense of manhood – to attain to a sense of stable masculine gender identity? Why so much male posturing, risk-taking, testing and competitive behaviour? A further related question is: Why do so many men, almost regardless of age, still struggle with achieving a settled and satisfactory sense of being a 'real' man? These are complex questions, the answers to which are crucial to understanding male psychology and the wider social relations played out between men and women.

Manhood, far from being simply anatomical maleness, a natural condition, or a state achieved through biological maturation is rather:

> *...a precarious or artificial state that boys must win against powerful odds.[4] ...it is a critical threshold that boys must pass through testing.[5]*

The notion of manhood is not only evident (with varying degrees of emphasis) in all known cultures, it is also observable across all socio-economic types and levels of socio-cultural development – irrespective of what other roles are recognised.

The demands of womanhood simply aren't comparable with those of manhood. Certainly, femininity is attained by girls (and women) through certain forms of social approval, but not to the same degree or in the same way as for boys (and men). Femininity is more qualified by sexual allure, body ornament, or:

> *...other essentially cosmetic behaviours that enhance, rather than create, an inherent quality of character. An authentic femininity rarely involves tests or proofs of action, or confrontation with dangerous foes: win-or-lose contests dramatically played out on the public stage. Rather than a critical threshold passed by traumatic testing, an either/or condition, femininity is more often construed as a biological given that is culturally refined or augmented.*[6]

A useful explanation of the different developmental demands placed on males and females in order to attain to acceptable adult status is available from the *post-Freuden ego psychology* attributable to Erik Erikson, Ralph Greenson, Edith Jacobson, Margaret Mahler, Gregory Rochlin, Robert Stoller, and D. W. Winnicott. According to this school of thought, infants (male and female) establish both a bond and a primary identity with their nurturing mother. An early and protracted 'psychic merging' with the mother marks a time when the infant does not distinguish between self and mother. Despite a physical separation of child and mother at birth, no equivalent psychological separation is effected. In time, the growing child attains the 'critical threshold' of 'separation-individuation', at which point its emerging awareness of 'psychic separateness' from the mother, combined with more developed motor skills and mobility, result in an enhanced capacity for independent action. Independent actions are socially reinforced in order that the child grows up. Though children of both genders experience these 'trial stages' of development, in which they are rewarded for gender appropriate behaviour, it is the male children who encounter special problems that hinder their progress toward 'independent selfhood'.[7]

> *The special liability for boys is the different fate of the primal psychic unity with the mother. The self-awareness of being a separate individual carries with it a parallel sense of a gender identity – being a man or a woman, boy or girl. In most societies, each individual must choose one or the other unequivocally in order, also, to be a separate and autonomous person recognisable as such by peers and thus to earn acceptance. The special problem the boy faces at this point is in overcoming the previous sense of unity with the mother in order to achieve an independent identity defined by his culture as masculine – an effort functionally equivalent not only to psychic separation but also to creating an autonomous public persona. The girl does not experience this problem as acutely, according to this theory, because her femininity is reinforced by her original symbiotic unity with her mother, by the identification with her that precedes self-identity and that culminates with her own motherhood (Chodorow 1978). In most societies, the little boy's sense of self as independent must include a sense of the self as different from his mother, as separate from her in ego-identity and in social role. Thus for the boy the task of separation and individuation carries an added burden and peril.[8]*

Masculinity and manhood, new and independent status, emerge only if the boy satisfies the test of breaking his bonds with his mother, making his own way in the world, and entering into 'a new and independent social status recognised as distinct and opposite from hers'.[9] But there is a persistent danger, 'an ambivalent fantasy-fear about the mother. The ineradicable fantasy is to return to the primal maternal symbiosis. The inseparable fear is that restoring the oneness with the mother will overwhelm one's independent selfhood'.[10] To the extent that he is drawn back toward mother and childhood, he is drawn away from the call and social expectation of autonomous manhood:

> *The struggle for masculinity is a battle against these regressive wishes and fantasies, a hard-fought renunciation of the longings for the prelapsarian idyll of childhood.*[11]

Manhood ideals and imagery then, in the post-Freudian perspective, serve as a defence against 'the eternal child within, against puerility'.[12]

The function of manhood ideals is not only individual but also social:

> *...regression is unacceptable not only to the individual but also to his society as a functioning mechanism, because most societies demand renunciation of escapist wishes in favour of a participating, contributing adult.*[13]

It is not hard to imagine the acute loneliness, insecurity and lostness of so many contemporary adolescent males, who must suffer not only the severe demands of individuation, but most often without any effective rights of passage, male role models or mentors who can 'show the way' and provide emotional and psychological support during such a turbulent and potentially traumatic transition from boyhood to manhood.

What also needs to be understood is that Manhood is always uncertain or precarious:

> *A prize to be won or wrested through struggle.*[14]

But why is this so? Manhood is a powerful ideal, imposed on males to ensure that they carry out their necessary roles. It is what is 'promised' to men for the performance of their roles. As well, it is what forces men:

> *...to shape up on penalty of being robbed of their identity, a threat apparently worse than death.*[15]

In any society where manhood is emphasised, an 'imperative triad' of moral injunctions appears to be evident: the expectation to impregnate women, to defend and protect dependants, and to provision one's family. Such men are expected to perform well beyond the simple Western mythology of breadwinner – they are expected to subdue and harness nature, to ensure the recreation and perpetuity of the basic building blocks of society ...to 'create something of value from nothing'. Manhood is likened to 'a kind of male procreation', heroic in the singularity of its disciplined and self-reliant autonomy.[16]

Compelled by 'moral codes and norms of culture', men are obliged, through psychological and material reward and punishment, to conduct their role not, as some people have assumed, for their own self-fulfilment and self-aggrandisement, but to ensure the replication of society's essential primary structures – chief amongst which is family. Without family no means exist for the perpetuation of culture.[17]

Manhood is a 'mythic confabulation that sanctifies male constructivity', ensuring that a boy will go on or grow up to produce and contribute to society more than he takes. It is society's necessary defence against 'entropy, human enemies, the forces of nature, time, and all the human weaknesses that endanger group life'. It reflects the mutualism that exists 'between a society's material context and its ideology, and between individual agency and structural constraint'.[18]

Serving these same ends, manhood ideology is a defence against 'psychic regression'; men must be prevented from taking a way of escape, or avoiding the responsibilities of manhood, by seeking solace in the maternal symbiosis of a prior infantile state of development. And why shouldn't men wish to resile from the 'imperative triad' through regression, given that in most societies its demands place men in serious confrontation and competition with their fellows, and in life threatening situations such as in battle. Anthropologist David Gilmore, has argued that, the imperatives of masculine destiny allow few men the indulgence of regression:

> *Because of the universal urge to flee from danger, we may regard "real" manhood as an inducement for high performance in the social struggle for scarce resources, a code of conduct that advances collective interests by overcoming inner inhibitions. In fulfilling their obligations, men stand to lose – a hovering threat that separates them from women, and boys. They stand to lose their reputation or their lives; yet their prescribed tasks must be done if the group is to survive and prosper. Because boys must steel themselves to enter into such struggles, they must be prepared by various sorts of tempering and toughening. To be men, most of all they must accept the fact that they are expendable. This acceptance of expendability constitutes the basis of the manly pose everywhere it is encountered; yet simple acquiescence will not do. To be socially meaningful, the decision for manhood must be characterised by enthusiasm combined with stoic resolve or perhaps "grace". It must show a public demonstration of positive choice, of jubilation even in pain, for it represents a moral commitment to defend the society and its core values against all odds.*[19]

Manhood ideologies are directly related to the expectations made on the male role. The harder, more threatening, competitive, or dangerous life is, the more stress will be placed on the manly ideal.

Manhood properly understood bespeaks the 'qualitative

nature of the masculine contribution' – contrary to the conventional and negative view that femininity is nurturant and passive compared with masculinity which is self-serving, uncaring and egotistical.

Manhood ideologies not only demand sacrificial self-giving but 'real' men are characterised by generosity, service, giving more than they take. And, though it may be less demonstrative and less direct and immediate than female giving, male giving is likewise nurturing. This is often passed over because male giving (and nurture) is comparatively obscure. It is focussed more on externals; the 'other' is not so much individual as collective – society. Men nurture their society (endowing and increasing) by steeling themselves against danger, through their productive effort, by fathering children and, if necessary, by dying. They are nurturing by exhibiting qualities that are the paradoxical opposite of those normally the measure of nurture; to support the family they may have to go away to work or war; to be tender and gentle they must have the hardness and strength to deal with enemies; to love they must be persistent and 'aggressive' enough to compete for a wife.[20]

We may summarise then that the manhood ideal, though rooted in and in continuity with biological masculinity, is therefore:

> *not purely psychogenetic in origin but is also a culturally imposed ideal to which men must conform whether or not they find it psychologically congenial.*[21]

Brief Profile of Contemporary Manhood

- When biologically innate masculinity (with its particular capacities, abilities, orientation and behaviours) is shaped by and made specific to a particular cultural/environmental setting, manhood is the outcome or product.
- Manhood is not anatomical maleness or a natural condition; it is not the result of biological maturation. It is a dynamic and precarious state that boys must win through testing and against powerful odds.
- Manhood is observable in all known cultures, and across all socio-economic types and levels of socio-cultural development – irrespective of what other roles are recognised.
- The developmental demands for boys and girls in making the transition into independent selfhood or adulthood are different. The special problem for boys is that they must (unlike girls) overcome their previous sense of unity with mother in order to achieve an independent masculine identity. This involves both psychic separation and the creation of an autonomous public persona. For boys the tasks of separation combined with individuation carry an added burden.
- Manhood only emerges if a boy satisfies the test of breaking bonds with his mother, making his own way in the world, and entering into 'a new and independent social status recognised as distinct and opposite from mother.' To the extent that he is drawn back to mother and childhood, he is drawn away and shrinks from the call and social expectation of autonomous manhood.
- The function of manhood is not just individual it is social. Regression is unacceptable both for the individual, who would lose his sense of independent masculine self identity, and for society because society demands the renunciation of escapist wishes in order that he might take his place and fulfil his role as a participating, contributing adult.
- Manhood is always uncertain or precarious; it is a powerful ideal imposed on males to ensure that they carry out their necessary roles. It is what is 'promised' to men for the performance of their roles. Non-conformity carries a potential penalty of being robbed of masculine identity; a threat which for most men would be 'worse than death'. Men are compelled and obliged, through psychological and material reward and punishment, to conduct their role not, as some people have assumed, for their own self-fulfilment and self-

aggrandisement, but to ensure the replication of society's essential primary structures.

- In any society where manhood is emphasised, men are expected to father children, defend, protect, and provision dependants.
- Manhood ensures that a boy will go on or grow up to produce and contribute to society more than he takes. It is society's defence against entropy, enemies, adverse events and forces in the environment, time, and the human weaknesses that might endanger group life.
- Manhood guards against men entertaining any urge to flee from danger. It is an inducement for men to perform well in the social struggle for scarce resources; it advances collective material and physical interests by ensuring that men overcome inner inhibitions.
- Though men stand to lose their reputation – even their lives in some circumstances, their tasks must be performed if society is to survive and prosper. Boys must steel themselves and be readied for this by tempering and toughening; because to be men they must accept that if a situation demands it, they are expendable.
- The emphasis placed on manhood is directly related to the demands made on the male role. The harder, more threatening, competitive, or dangerous life is, the more stress will be placed on the manly ideal.
- Manhood not only demands sacrificial self-giving, but 'real' men must give more than they take. And, though it may appear less demonstrative, direct and immediate than female giving, male giving is likewise nurturing. Male giving may appear less conspicuous because it is focussed more on externals or the collective rather than the individual. Men nurture society in a myriad of ways, through their productive efforts, by steeling themselves against danger and hazards, by fathering children, and if necessary by dying. They are nurturant in ways that are indispensable, yet which do not usually draw attention to themselves or generate feelings of rapport, closeness or gratefulness.
- Though rooted in masculine biology, manhood is not only psychogenetic, it is a culturally imposed ideal to which men must conform irrespective of whether or not they find it congenial.

Table 5

'NORMATIVE MALE ALEXITHYMIA' THE NEW CATCH PHRASE FOR MALE PATHOLOGY

Normative male alexithymia is the fashionable term gaining increasing popularity as a way of describing a fundamental problem with masculine gender and the social conditioning that (it is claimed) originates and reinforces it. The assumptions this term represents are central to recent 'textbook' models for understanding male psychology and for practising psychotherapy. Though these models are touted as 'new', disappointingly they largely represent an outmoded and discredited gender politics, clothed and articulated in a somewhat 'new' way, to appeal to the emerging interest in men's issues. That some of the ideas of these models are both misleading and yet not entirely without some merit, demands their brief analysis.

The term alexithymia refers to the inability to put emotions into words. As a clinical definition it has been used to describe the psychopathology of severe emotional constriction (originally in psychosomatic, drug dependent Post-Traumatic Stress Disorder).[22] More recently, the term has been used to describe mild to moderate forms of emotional constriction, associated with emotion suppression and inexpressivity, a 'phemomenon' claimed to be normative amongst men and highly problematical for their psychological well-being. This allegedly widespread problem has been termed (most conspicuously in profeminist literature) as *normative male alexithymia.*[23/24]

One of the best known promoters of this term and the assumptions it describes is Ronald Levant (co-author of the book *New Psychotherapy For Men*), who suggests that the condition of normative male alexithymia arises as a consequence of the trauma associated with the male role socialisation process; and that this trauma is so normative it is not thought of as trauma at all.[25]

Whilst Levant states that it is not his intention to use this term to pathologise men or males, he quite clearly does pathologise the gender characteristics and socialisation associated with masculinity, and promotes a profeminist social constructionist two domain sex/gender ideology.

Despite Levant's overly laboured and elaborated view of normative male emotional ill-health, it is probably true to say that some males are significantly traumatised by the whole process of male role socialisation; not because toughness, self-denial, self-reliance, autonomy and public emotional inexpressiveness are emphasised, but because too often these gender characteristics are over-emphasised or emphasised to the exclusion of, or in the absence of, other essential masculine gender attributes   (a topic to be examined more fully later).

Trauma as a result of an inappropriate emphasis or imbalance of gender role socialisation may indeed occur, and give rise to problems such as rigid and global emotional inexpressivity and very unhealthy and self-defeating emotional constriction. But to suggest that men's lesser (on average) ability and inclination to verbally and publicly express emotions compared to women's, and men's tendency to prefer a different strategy for emotion regulation to women, represent the negative effects of socialisation trauma, and a normative incapacity and dysfunction, is plainly contrary to evidence, and simply serves to reinforce a deficit image of men. It also legitimises the deleterious anti-male propaganda calling for the demasculinisation and feminisation of men and boys.

Levant makes a number of assertions (associated with the idea of normative male alexithymia) that are important for us to consider critically. He argues that:

- A consequence of the 'male role socialisation ordeal' is

that, 'boys grow up to be men who are genuinely unaware of their emotions, and sometimes even their body sensations'.[26] Men do not give a direct account of their emotions as women do, 'they tend to rely on their cognition to deduce logically what they should feel under the circumstances'; 'they cannot do what is easy and almost automatic for most women – simply direct their senses inward, feel the feeling and let the verbal description come to mind'.[27]

- The apparent inability of men to readily identify and verbally express emotions prevents them 'from utilising the most effective means known for dealing with life stresses and traumas – namely identifying, thinking about, and discussing one's emotional responses to a stressor or trauma, with a friend, family member or therapist'.[28] This (Levant argues) predisposes men to 'deal with stress in ways that make certain forms of pathology more likely, such as substance abuse, violent behaviour, sexual compulsions, stress-related illnesses, and early death. It also makes it less likely that such men will be able to benefit from psychotherapy as traditionally practised'.[29]

- Mild alexithymia as a feature of traditional masculinity 'does not serve men well in today's world, and is therefore dysfunctional, although it did serve a purpose in earlier historical eras'.[30] 'Traditional masculinity ideology fits better with harsh social conditions, such as occurred in… (U.S.A) from the period of industrialisation through the great depression and the two World Wars'.[31]

Undoubtedly, some boys do grow up to be men who are unaware of their emotions and sometimes even their body sensations. And though this may well be due to problems of masculine socialisation, the fact that some females experience similar difficulties suggests that other factors, such as childhood circumstances or neurodevelopmental factors, may also figure prominently. Even if it can be demonstrated that *some* boys do, as a result of masculine socialisation, experience difficulties in relation to emotion expression and recognition of body sensations later in life, to extrapolate that this is a normative male phenomenon is illegitimate.

Levant rightly observes that men do not express their emotions as women do; nor do they do what is 'easy and almost automatic for most women': feel feelings and 'let the verbal description come to mind'. Men tend not to do these things as women do simply because they are not women. Men's sex-specific cognitive and expressive orientation, rooted in biology and reinforced and elaborated by cultural expectations and conditioning, causes men to conduct their emotional lives differently to women. And it is precisely on this point that Levant departs from the available evidence of gender psychology, preferring the two domain sex/gender theory of profeminist social constructionism. In support of another author (J. Pleck, originator of the *Gender Role Strain Theory*), he states that masculinity and femininity are not the same thing as, 'nor are they essential to, being male or female respectively'; '...these definitions of gender (are) historically relative and socially constructed'.[32]

Levant's assertion that men's emotional inexpressiveness and more limited emotional faculty (compared with women) prevents them from coping effectively, again, does not take account of men's and women's characteristically different coping styles and behaviours, or the biological imperatives or social role demands that both shape and necessitate them. And, whilst it appears to be the case that global suppression, emotional inexpressiveness and constriction *may* render *some* men more prone to substances abuse, violent behaviour, sexual compulsions, stress-related illnesses and early death, this should not be taken to suggest straightforward causality. Furthermore, other potential contributory causal factors merit consideration, such as hormonal, occupational and socio-economic factors. Any simplistic linking of masculine gender with problems experienced by a small number of men is more the subjective stance of ideology than a correlation supported by data.

As for the claim that mild alexithymia 'does not serve men well in today's world, and is therefore dysfunctional, although it did serve a purpose in earlier historical eras': as we have observed, the emphasis placed on the manhood ideal does tend to be more pronounced in more difficult, dangerous and demanding times and circumstances. And it follows that the need for stricter emotion regulation for the performance of male roles would also be more greatly needed – and would reflect in the nature of role socialisation. However, to suggest that life is now so easy that the manhood ideal can be dispensed with, is not only a myopic misreading of local and global societal realities, it is also a simplistic trivialisation of the complex nature of manhood. Not only is manhood rooted in and inseparable from sex-specific male physiology, it is essential to both human survival and the affluence, stability and security Western men *and* women have come to demand. Furthermore, no matter what its problems and excesses (which we must seek to remedy), the manhood ideal is reflected in and integral to a myriad of social, economic and political institutions, and, though varying in emphasis at different times and in different circumstances of societal need, for the foreseeable future its role is indispensable, and its continuity inevitable.

Normative Male Alexithymia?

- Normative male alexithymia is a term that has become popular as a way of emphasising what is believed by some to be the flawed nature of male role socialisation. The term describes mild to moderate forms of emotional constriction associated with emotional suppression and inexpressivity. It is alleged that this is a widespread 'normative' male problem and condition, and that it arises as a consequence of the trauma of male role socialisation.

- It is probably true to say that some males are traumatised by the process of male role socialisation, not because toughness, self-denial, self-reliance, autonomy and public emotional inexpressiveness are emphasised, but because these characteristics may be overemphasised or emphasised to the exclusion of or in the absence of other essential masculine gender attributes.

- Such trauma may occur and result in rigid and global emotional inexpressiveness and very unhealthy and self-defeating emotional constriction. However, to suggest that men's lesser ability and tendency to express emotions compared to women's, and men's tendency to prefer a different strategy of emotion regulation (compared to women) represents the negative effects of socialisation trauma, and is a normative problem, is plainly contrary to evidence. This view serves to reinforce a deficit image of men, and promotes the derogatory idea that men need to be demasculinised and feminised.

- To suggest that life is now so easy that the manhood ideal can be dispensed with is both naïve (given local and global societal realities), and a simplistic trivialisation of the complex nature of manhood.

- The notion of normative male alexithymia, its generalisation of the problems of a small number of men to *all* men, and its inference pathologising manhood and masculine role socialisation, is much more a construct of ideology than evidence.

Table 6

IN DEFENCE OF 'ACTION EMPATHY'

In addition to 'normative male alexithymia', Levant believes that the consequences of male role socialisation – in particular 'emotion socialisation', are evident in men's use of 'action empathy' rather than empathy.[33]

Empathy has been defined as 'interpersonal understanding'.[34] This means 'stepping aside', or thinking outside one's own frame of reference, and making an effort to understand or at least appreciate another person's perspective and experience – including feelings.[35]

Levant contends that men are apt to employ an inferior form of empathy, which he terms *action empathy*, which is more about making predictions concerning what another person will do or should do. According to Levant, it aims not to know how another person feels for their benefit, but rather is often in some way self-serving, such as 'sizing-up' a competitor; it is therefore not usually pro-social as is empathy. He suggests that action empathy is usually:

> *...learned... on the playing fields, from gym teachers and sports coaches, who put a premium on learning an opponent's general approach, strengths, weaknesses and body language, in order to figure out how he might react in a given situation.*[36]

This sizing-up behaviour (which Levant views negatively), is actually in many contexts a useful and appropriate behaviour. And, though it may be used inappropriately in a self-serving way, used appropriately it is clearly pro-social, such as in many activities associated with law enforcement, defence, politics and commerce. In fact, it is indispensable to the 'imperative triad' of expectations: to succeed in securing a mate/partner, to defend and protect dependants, and to provision one's family and community. As already noted, Manhood (with its many uncongenial expectations), demands of men that they contend with many competitive and oppositional forces; it demands sacrificial self-giving which, though less demonstrative and less direct and immediate than female giving, is no less important or nurturing – a reality all too easily overlooked.[37]

Certainly, the behaviour to which Levant refers may be used selfishly or inappropriately in relation to others who are in need of interpersonal understanding. And it may well be that men are perhaps more likely to misuse this behaviour than women. However, men are by no means alone in using insensitive, exploitative or self-serving behaviours in interpersonal relationships.

'Taking another person's perspective and being able to know how they feel' may not come as naturally to men as it does to women; nor is this likely to be a man's 'default tendency', but that doesn't mean men can't have (or attain) empathy, or that they choose not to be empathic when to do so is of significant importance. It also needs to be said that empathy in circumstances that call for sizing-up behaviour (or Levant's *action empathy*) is no less unhelpful and inappropriate than sizing-up behaviour in an interpersonal relationship that is in need of empathy.

Achieving interpersonal understanding has some obvious potential benefits. That we feel or sense that someone else understands us and something of our experience may be very helpful. Empathy can provide an important basis for moral action. It can also be personally transformative, because it can challenge us and move us to permit and embrace important changes in our thinking and behaviour. Yet in some circumstances it can serve to be little more than a self-gratifying and morally redundant form of emotional voyeurism. Empathy without appropriate action, if action is called for, is little better than sympathy. To achieve an understanding of another's experience, to 'know' how they feel and to 'feel with them', may be meaningless without practical action. For example, achieving empathy in relation to a person who is grief-stricken by bereavement may have little value on its own, if what that person most needs is practical assistance with burdensome tasks.

Author Patrick West, in his recent book *Conspicuous Compassion*, cautions against the popular tendency to elevate feeling and caring as virtuous ends in themselves. He observes that much public 'caring' behaviour is more about feeling good, not doing good. 'The three C's of modern life – compassion, caring and crying in public – show not how altruistic we have become, but how selfish'.[38] Doing good may sometimes not feel good at all; it may be an emotionally colourless and inexpressive purposive act of will, borne out in concrete actions aimed at another's (or others') betterment. There is an argument here to suggest more careful discernment about men's responses which in some circumstances, though action oriented, practical and inexpressive of emotion, may in fact be well informed with understanding and charged with compassionate concern. And it would seem reasonable to infer that sometimes genuinely compassionate behaviour has been undervalued for no other reason than its inconspicuous emotionality.

Action Empathy and Doing Good

- The term 'Action Empathy' has been proposed as a term to describe an inferior form of empathy, which is about making predictions concerning what another person will do or should do; it is about sizing-up a competitor, to figure out how he might react in a given situation.

- Though some men may use this behaviour selfishly or inappropriately in interpersonal relationships, both men *and* women sometimes use exploitative and self-serving behaviours unhelpful to relationships.

- The 'sizing-up' behaviour of 'Action Empathy' is in many contexts (in which male roles are performed) actually useful, appropriate, and pro-social (such as, law enforcement, defence, politics, and commerce).

- Manhood, with its many uncongenial expectations, demands of men that they contend with many competitive and oppositional forces.

- Though empathy (taking another's perspective and being able to know how they feel) may not come as naturally to men as it does to women, men can and do have (and attain) empathy when to do so is of significant importance.

- Empathy in circumstances that call for 'sizing-up' behaviour is no less unhelpful or inappropriate than 'sizing-up' behaviour in an interpersonal relationship that is in need of empathy.

- Though empathy may have a number of potential benefits, in some circumstances (particularly when understanding *and* action is needed) it may serve to be little more than self-gratifying and morally redundant.

- Doing good may not feel good at all; it may be a purposive act of will, borne out in concrete actions.

- Compassionate behaviour has often been undervalued for no other reason than its inconspicuous emotionality.

Table 7

BECOMING A MAN – THINGS THAT CAN GO WRONG

As we have noted, the process of masculine socialisation and male development prepares boys for the difficult and demanding roles they may be called upon to perform in the world of men. Far from straightforward or congenial, this process has suffering for most boys, but for some, particularly if they are ill-suited to the demands of the manhood ideal, the experience can be a markedly traumatic one. Some boys may be left negatively affected and diminished in their capacity to conduct their emotional lives, relationships and sexuality in ways that are functional, adaptive and helpful to themselves and others.

However unpalatable, the reality we cannot deny is that the manhood ideal to which men must conform will persist. And though varying in emphasis (depending on circumstances and need), its potential to reward and punish, enhance or diminish boys and men will also persist. Fortunately, at least in complex Western society, the demands of manhood, though inescapably uncongenial, are for many ameliorated by liberal social and occupational arrangements, accommodating of those least suited to the 'rough and tumble' of the more traditional interpretations of masculinity. And this is surely a civilising feature of any society; a feature to be valued, reinforced and preserved. But alongside this important accommodation (and in no way diminishing it) we must consider carefully the consequences of not adequately preparing boys for the demands that will be made on them by a society (whatever its current whims and fancies), that still subscribes to gender roles, because it needs to, prefers to, and simply must. However, what is observable at the group level should not be taken to mean that any single individual, whether male or female, should necessarily feel limited or restricted in the performance of any task or in the pursuit of any goal. Nor should what we generally observe about gender and gender role orientations be taken to support any facile generalisations that seek to cement negative stereotypes of either sex.[39] And though we must acknowledge the necessity of the manhood ideal if we are to survive and to continue to experience the kind of social order we have become accustomed to and demand, there is, nevertheless, much scope and need to acknowledge what is problematic with male socialisation, but only within a framework that acknowledges and values its utility. Some of the things that can go wrong and things which are currently deficient in this process we will now consider.

Intimacy and Sexuality

For some boys grappling with the whole business of growing up, there is too little scope within their social environment and social learning and conditioning to gain appropriate skills, awareness and consideration of other adult intimate relationships. If during their passage toward adulthood they experience (and assimilate as normative) an overemphasis on emotional inexpressiveness and suppression, and on hiding all signs of softness and vulnerability in nearly all rather than some circumstances, they may find it very difficult in adult life both to engage and work with their emotional experiences (including caring for their own emotional and physical needs) and to participate in healthy intimacy. They may be retarded in their ability to get their own intimacy needs met in an appropriate way, as well as proving to be a frustration and disappointment to later female partners who anticipate reciprocal intimacy.[40]

These same over-emphases of inexpressiveness and suppression may also result in male over-dependence on women (and female partners) later in life for emotional nurture, a sense of emotional well-being, emotional expressiveness, and physical care.[41/42] A global unacceptability of expressing or exhibiting affectionate emotions or 'caring/connection emotions' may result in these emotions being channelled into sexuality. This, combined with immature notions of adolescent sexuality of 'scoring' and performance as trophies of masculine adequacy, may result in sexuality and sexual experience becoming an overburdened vehicle for expressing intimacy and meeting intimacy needs. And, as Levant suggests:

> *Fuelled by the hormonal changes that accompany puberty... this often takes the form of non-relational sexuality or unconnected lust.[43]*

The combining of status behaviour, hormonally fuelled sexual desire and intimacy needs, into sexual behaviour and expectation, may result in insensitive behaviour counter productive to a relationship, or, alternatively, the frivolous exploitation of intimate female sexual partners (who may be simply discarded or used); at worst this combination may manifest in inappropriate or even harmfully aggressive sexual behaviour.

Overdeveloped Anger

A further potential consequence of the emphasis in male socialisation on emotional inexpressiveness and suppression is, according to Levant, the overdevelopment of anger. Men tend to express anger more aggressively than do women; that is, as a 'motor/behavioural response'. Vulnerable emotions like hurt, shame, disappointment and fear, 'get funnelled into the anger channel', that 'final common pathway' for emotions that are felt to be 'too unmanly to express directly'.[44] Levant identifies two further anger phenomena: some men *actively transform* vulnerable emotions into anger, like when a boy is pushed to the ground and determines to get back up showing no weakness or emotion except anger to defy an aggressor; many men fail to recognise anger in its milder forms (such as irritation or annoyance), which may give rise to angry outbursts. This has been termed the 'rubber band syndrome'.[45/46]

There is little doubt that these behavioural phenomena appear to be associated with traditional male socialisation, but of a kind that carries an *over-emphasis* on emotional inexpressiveness and suppression, in relation to (or because of the absence of) other essential counter-balancing masculine attributes. And though men may certainly be observed to exhibit angry outbursts, described as the 'rubber band syndrome', both this and somewhat similar *passive-aggressive* behaviour are arguably not gender specific in their prevalence. It is also important to reiterate here that couple's communication and conflict research indicates that, in interpersonal interactions and partner relationships, women not men have been found to exhibit most anger.[47/48/49/50]

Defensive Behaviours

As we have observed, the demands of manhood exhorted through the tasks and emphases of boyhood development and socialisation oblige boys to avoid things conspicuously feminine, and to draw away from dependent ties with mother, as means of achieving independent male/masculine status. However, if these demands are not balanced with adequate opportunities for the safe acknowledgement and expression of fear, inadequacy, fragility and vulnerability – in a male appropriate environment – rigid, immature and unhelpful defensive behaviours may take shape and persist into later life. Perhaps most common are the defences of emphatic self-sufficiency, avoidance of attachment and commitment, and projection.

Males generally need to achieve a degree of toughness, stoicism and self-sufficiency – because that is what male roles often demand. But this can be taken too far. Males who overemphasise self-sufficiency, often do so while unknowingly relying too heavily on an intimate female partner. In its worst form, this unwitting emotional dependence can become a cause of neurotic and overbearing control which, in turn, can set the relationship on a disastrous course.

The issue of separation from mother (breaking dependent ties) may also be found connected with overemphasised self-sufficiency and dependence. If yearning for a 'lost' mother is ineffectually resolved, and hidden from awareness, it may well be transferred to a female partner – who becomes a mother substitute.

However, for fear of appearing vulnerable, weak or dependent, some men may deny their partners any mutually empathic response, and they may withhold commitment or relational ties for fear of evoking and re-experiencing the unresolved grief, emotional pain and sadness of estrangement – or risking a re-run of their former experience of separation/'abandonment'. Having little or no insight into the contradictoriness of strongly professing self-sufficiency, whilst actually being dependent, may be a source of internal conflict.

Emotional dependence on a partner may at some level be experienced as powerlessness, being 'at their mercy', which might generate anger and resentment whose origins are imperceptible and consequently, in their expression in a relationship, are problematic. These kinds of dynamics may combine with the experience of a traumatic separation from mother, to generate fear, mistrust or dislike of women.

The most common and quite evident problem with male over-dependence (emotionally) on female partners is the dysregulating and sometimes explosive potential of such relationships in the event of their breakdown (which is also common and understandable because of how stifling and burdensome the weight of dependence can be). If such a relationship begins to falter, the equilibrium of the dependent individual may be put sorely under threat; it may force exposure of dependence, produce a reaction of anticipatory grief, or strong feelings of powerlessness – all potentially giving rise to anger. Great fear of shame (particularly the shame of exhibiting emotional vulnerability), or feelings of hurt, pain and powerlessness, may be funnelled into the one undifferentiated emotion of anger and in some circumstances rage.

Though in no way justifying anger that is expressed through aggressive or violating behaviour, there is much scope for educating men and women, and human service workers, about how to appropriately respond to men experiencing problematic anger. Though anger is certainly a predictor of aggression, it often needlessly leads to aggression because it is not engaged by others with any attempt at understanding, and is often exacerbated and amplified by being ignored, rejected, or competitively confronted and challenged. Forced to turn in on itself (rather than being thoughtfully engaged and defused) it tends to escalate through self-fuelling. And yet, as we have already noted, differentiated emotions and their meaning are often available 'behind' the presentation of anger.

Again associated with an over-emphasis on self-sufficiency, and a fear of vulnerability and inadequacy of dependence, some men clearly exhibit avoidance of attachment and commitment, in case they are thought to be dependent, needy, or given to what might be seen as characteristically feminine relationship seeking behaviour. Unfortunately, this can mean that opportunities for relationship are forgone or spoiled, and much needed and potentially beneficial relational ties are not formed – exacerbating loneliness and neediness, and reinforcing the tendency to retreat into illusory self-sufficiency.

Associated and converging with the defensive behaviours already mentioned may be *projection* – that is, the tendency to project one's own 'out of awareness' and rejected vulnerabilities, neediness and insecurities onto a female partner. Some men appear to select a female partner who is a mirror image of themselves – or at least has similar vulnerabilities and dependency issues; a partner who may invest themselves in the relationship to the neglect of their own development and, in the long-run, their own wellbeing.[51]

This form of projection may encourage an orientation of personality that is not only self-convincingly self-sufficient but may also tend to be narcissistic, self-centred, emotionally distant and aloof – while actually protecting against deep feelings of inadequacy, shame, dependency, fragility, and neediness. Projecting these largely unrecognised elements of emotional content onto a female partner, and using her to provide an alternative emotional centre for one's own emotionally fragile existence, is fraught with problems.[52/53]

A man in such a relationship may experience much mistrust and insecurity with a 'need' to control his female partner and lock her into a comparatively dependent, devalued, and severely inhibited role, in order to minimise any threat to his emotional stability. Such a relationship, in which a female partner is burdened with a man's projections, and which is rigidly closed and contained by the insecurity and dependence that are primary to it, has a considerable likelihood of self-destructing. Moreover, individual personalities in this context may well be moulded to be maladaptive and vulnerable to any number of common negative major life events.

Depression

A belief aligned with pro-feminist social constructionism is that traditional male socialisation results in the male self being structured and resting on faulty psychic foundations; with the masculine gender identity having at its core an ungrieved abandonment depression.[54] This phenomenon is believed in part to reflect the consequence of self-reproach which originates from an inversion of unconscious criticism against the mother from whom a boy was traumatically separated.[55] However, in all the commentary on this alleged 'epidemic' of abandonment depression, no-one appears to take account of the potential depressant effects of men and boys being pushed into existential crisis by the ideological negation of masculinity and manhood, or the conflicting and confusing societal role demands (also ideologically driven), that result in profound self-devaluation.

Though *some* men may indeed harbour and suffer from depression associated with an ungrieved abandonment or problematic separation from mother, assertions about faulty psychic foundations or abandonment depression being a core feature of masculine gender identity in general are reductionist, forced, and appear to 'play to the gallery' of profeminist bias.

Yet despite these issues of contention, depression is a problem amongst men; it causes great suffering, and though more than twice as many women compared to men suffer depression the gap between the sexes appears to be narrowing.[56] It has been argued that depression in some men is masked by substance abuse (whereas women are more likely to exhibit a comorbid pattern with anxiety – i.e. depression and anxiety together); also, that this difference is not well identified using present diagnostic tools.[57] It is further conjectured that, as a consequence, more men suffer from depression than previously thought. Denial, soldiering on, not communicating publicly how they feel or what they are experiencing, and the unpreparedness (or inability) of clinicians to get beyond male defences may, it is suggested, be preventing detection and diagnosis.[58]

Much depression in men *and* women goes undetected and undiagnosed – suggesting the need for caution in conjecturing about comparative prevalence with improved detection and diagnosis. Nevertheless, a significant number of men do experience depression (and the incidence is rising), and better prevention and early intervention efforts are needed. And though the current comparative prevalence of depression (by sex) appears to favour greater resources focussing on women, two important factors need to be taken into consideration: firstly, men of all age groups in Australia are far more likely than women to die from suicide – more women deliberately self-harm and attempt suicide than men, but men are four times more likely than women to succeed;[59] secondly, depression is associated with two major physical health issues for men – hypertension, and heart disease, with a 60% greater incidence of hypertension, and a four-fold greater risk for myocardial infarction for patients who are depressed.[60/61]

It has been important to acknowledge that, though we cannot dispense with the manhood ideal or with male gender role socialisation, there are casualties of the process of boys being prepared for the world of men, and there is much need for us to examine and rectify the deficiencies in this process. Yet without in any way compromising this essential endeavour (something that will be examined at length later), it needs to be said that not all men, or most men, but rather a minority of men experience the *severe* problems that may result from a traumatic male role socialisation process.

ROLES IN PERSPECTIVE

Historically, women and men have always had to grapple with shaping their roles and everyday responsibilities to suit the changing demands and circumstances of workplace, environment and society. And whilst people everywhere strive to achieve quality of life, for the majority survival still remains the focus and priority of daily life. As affluent Westerners, we have increasingly experienced the luxury of freedoms and choices unimaginable for most other people in the world. We are able to entertain refinements in culture and social relations unthinkable for some societies – such as exploring more diverse and flexible roles, and changes in expectations about intimacy, love the general quality of interpersonal interactions, communication and sharing. Yet this environment with its many liberties, in which we luxuriate and which we jealously guard, did not happen by chance – it was achieved (and is maintained) in significant measure by the industry, ingenuity, indomitable determination and sheer drivenness of men; men in service to the demands imposed by manhood ('to which men must conform whether or not they find it psychologically congenial').[62]

Men caught up in the ideal and in service to the demands of manhood have significantly shaped and furnished the milieu (albeit sometimes hesitantly) in which movements for social change have been permitted and have flourished – much as the women's movement which, quite rightly, sought for women equity, just consideration, and valued participation in the life and institutions of society. It is an irony that out of this setting should come such a negative view of men, and such an orchestrated attempt to repudiate masculinity. Certainly, the case can be made – and needs to be, for counterbalancing the excesses and problems associated with some current emphases apparent in male culture and male role socialisation, but to suggest, as gender feminist social constructionists do, that men's masculine roles are redundant and that we have now arrived at a point in social history permitting and necessitating men's feminisation and demasculinisation, is dangerously naïve.

We have noted that men and women (on average) exhibit comparative differences in their cognitive orientations, life and relational priorities, and characteristic ways of conducting their emotional lives. Men *and* women are the cause of perplexity and difficulties in relation to each other in attempting to achieve meaningful and workable intimate relationships. Berating men's ways of expressing love and intimacy, all too often simply obscures the reality of some women's difficulties in contributing to intimate relationships in an appropriate and mutually beneficial way. Feminine styles of loving (and measures of love) and preferences for intimacy do not represent an adequate definition of love and intimacy unless men's preferences and measures of these things are also included, such as:

– Sharing activities and tasks
– Giving practical help and support
– Sexual intimacy and physical affection
– The expression of positive feelings
– Protectiveness
– Industry, work, providing for partner and for a shared future.[63]

It goes without saying that men can learn to be better lovers, partners and companions – and it is in their best interests to do so. They need, as an integral element of male maturation, to be able to both regulate and 'work with' their emotional experience, and to learn a healthy degree of genuine emotional autonomy, avoiding being overly dependent on female partners, or using them to provide a centre for a fragile emotional existence. However, though our concern here is with much needed male maturation, and personal and interpersonal improvement, the same general emphasis is also relevant to women. They too can be inappropriately and inadequately prepared to contribute maturely and helpfully to intimate relationships. Women may also need to learn how to negotiate workable compromises in communication and meeting their personal needs; they too must achieve a balance between autonomy and dependence, and an understanding of their partner's ways of being, loving and contributing to relationship.

Finally, it is crucial to understand that if men are to be better partners, more balanced in their masculinity and healthy in the conduct of their emotional lives, this will not be achieved by diminishing manhood or manliness, or by brow beating men into mimicking female/feminine ways of being. To do so is counterproductive, inequitable and dehumanising.

Balance and psychological wholeness for men (if these are to be genuine) can only spring from and occur within the full repertoire of manly attributes associated with mature manhood; attributes which are often neglected or absent in contemporary male role socialisation. Men will never be like women (without our biology fundamentally changes), nor would women want them to be. Men do need to make room in their lives for and practise gentleness, attentiveness, sensuality and emotional expressiveness, but only in a way that is congruent and not at odds with the irreducible reality of masculinity and the fundamental elements of manhood – what men are and must be for all our sakes.

Having established a basis for understanding the particular developmental issues of manhood and the cultural imperatives that significantly shape it and place demands on it, in the following chapter we must explore and acknowledge one capacity for which manhood appears 'designed' and yet which can go badly wrong, and that is violence.

Male Role Socialisation - Potential Problems

For some boys (especially if they are ill-suited to the demands of the manhood ideal), the experience of masculine role socialisation may be traumatic. Some boys may be negatively affected in their capacity to conduct their emotional lives, relationships and sexuality in ways that are functional, adaptive and helpful to themselves and others.

Fortunately, in our society, though the demands of manhood are still inescapably uncongenial, we do have some social and occupational arrangements that are accommodating of those who are least suited to the 'rough and tumble' of the more traditional interpretations of masculinity.

Though we must prepare boys to enter the world of men, and though we must acknowledge the necessity of the manhood ideal, we need also to reckon with what is problematic within current male socialisation, and the kind of problems some boys may encounter in later adult life.

For boys who experience (and assimilate as normative) an overemphasis on emotional inexpressiveness and suppression, and on concealing all signs of softness and vulnerability in nearly all rather than some circumstances; and where this overemphasis predominates in relation to or because of the absence of other essential counterbalancing masculine attributes, the following problems *may* occur:

- Difficulty in later life engaging and working with their emotional experiences, and participating in healthy intimacy.

- May become over-dependent on women (and female partners) for emotional nurture and a sense of emotional well-being.

- 'Caring/connection emotions' may be channelled into sexuality; sexuality and sexual experience may become an overburdened vehicle for expressing intimacy and meeting intimacy needs (which may take the form of non-relational sexuality). This combined with status behaviour, may result in insensitive, exploitative or (in the extreme) even harmfully aggressive sexual behaviour.

- The overdevelopment of anger.

- The funnelling of vulnerable emotions (like, hurt, shame, disappointment and fear) into the anger 'channel'.

- The active transformation of vulnerable emotions into anger (such as in defiance of an aggressor).

- Failure to recognise anger in its milder forms (such as irritation or annoyance), consequenting angry outbursts (the 'rubber band syndrome').

If the tasks and emphases of boyhood development and socialisation (with the obligation to avoid things feminine and to separate from mother) are not balanced with adequate support and opportunities for the acknowledgement and expression of vulnerable emotions in a safe male-appropriate environment, unhelpful defensive behaviours may take shape and persist into later life, including:

- *Emphatic Self-Sufficiency* – while unknowingly relying too heavily on an intimate female partner. At worst this may be associated with anxious, neurotic, overbearing control. Emotional over-dependence on a partner may be experienced as powerlessness, being 'at their mercy'; which might generate resentment and anger with little or no insight into the reason for these emotions. In the event of its breakdown such a relationship has the potential to cause huge upheaval, emotional pain and a sense of powerlessness, which may in turn give rise to anger and an aggressive endeavour to restore equilibrium through control. Without insight about the underlying problem constructive problem solving is ineffectual.

- *Avoidance of attachment and commitment* – which may be associated with emphatic self-sufficiency, dependence, and the particular issue of separation from mother. If yearning for a 'lost' mother is ineffectually resolved it may be 'transferred' to a female partner – who becomes a mother substitute. Commitment and relational ties may be withheld for fear of evoking and re-experiencing unresolved grief, pain and sadness of estrangement – risking a re-run of the earlier experience of mother separation/'abandonment'. Avoidance of attachment and commitment may also be the effect of so rigidly avoiding being seen as in any way dependent, needy, or given to what might be considered as characteristically feminine relationship seeking behaviour.

- *Projection* – The tendency to project one's own 'out of awareness' and rejected vulnerabilities, neediness, and insecurities onto a female partner (possibly, though unknowingly selected for having similar vulnerabilities and dependency issues). Projecting these largely unrecognised elements of emotional content onto a female partner, and using her to provide an alternative emotional centre for one's own emotionally fragile existence, is fraught with problems. A man in such a relationship may experience much mistrust and insecurity, with a 'need' to control his female partner and lock her into a comparatively dependent, devalued, and severely inhibited role, in order to minimise any threat to his emotional stability. Such a relationship, in which a female partner is burdened with a man's projections, and which is rigidly closed and contained by the insecurity and dependence that are primary to it, has a considerable likelihood of self-destructing. Moreover, individual personalities in this context may well be moulded to be maladaptive and vulnerable to any number of common negative major life events.

Some pro-feminist authors believe that the masculine gender identity has at its core an ungrieved abandonment depression. A number of points need to be made in response to this belief:

- Though *some* men may experience an ungrieved abandonment depression, no evidence warrants this being said of all men.

- Conveniently overlooked in this view of men is any reckoning with the depressant effects of men and boys being actively undermined in achieving a meaningful self-identity, through attempts to demasculinise and feminise them. How telling are these factors in predisposing males to depression and self-reproach?

- Depression is a problem amongst men (though based on current statistics, is less so than amongst women), and its incidence is rising.

- Better diagnostic tools and clinical practices may assist in detecting depression in men. However, much depression in women *and* men goes undetected and undiagnosed – suggesting the need for caution in conjecturing about comparative prevalence with improved detection and diagnosis.

- Though present statistics on depression appear to favour a greater focus on depression in women, men are more likely to die from suicide, and depression in men is associated with a 60% greater incidence of hypertension, and a four-fold greater risk for myocardial infarction.

Not all men, or most men, but rather a minority of men experience the *severe* problems that *may* result from a traumatic male role socialisation process.

Table 8

References

1. See for example: Pollack, W. and Levant, R., **New Psychotherapy For Men** (New York, John Wiley and Sons, 1998)

2. Ashfield, J., **Gender, Masculinity and Manhood: Core Concepts For Understanding Men's Issues** (Western Australia, Ikon Institute, 2003), p. 117. *This Book has been revised and reissued under the title:* **The Making Of A Man: Reclaiming masculinity and manhood in the light of reason** *(South Australia, Peacock Publications, 2004)*

3. Ibid.

4. Gilmore, D., **Manhood In the Making** (U.S.A., Yale University Press, 1990) p. 11.

5. Ibid.

6. Ibid., p. 11 & 12

7. Op. cit., Ashfield, p. 42

8. Op. cit., Gilmore, p. 26 & 27

9. Ibid., p. 28

10. Ibid.

11. Ibid., p. 28 & 29

12. Ibid., p. 29

13. Ibid.

14. Ibid., p. 24

15. Ibid., p. 221

16. Ibid., p. 222 & 223

17. Ibid., p. 225

18. Ibid., p. 226

19. Ibid., p. 223 & 224

20. Ibid., p. 230

21. Ibid., p. 4 & 5

22. Sifneos, P., **Clinical Observations On Some Patients Suffering From A Variety Of Psychosomatic Diseases** *Proceedings of the Seventh European Conference On Psychosomatic Research* (Basel, Switzerland, 1967)

23. Levant, R. and Kopecky, G., **Masculinity Reconstructed** (New York, Dutton, 1995)

24. Pollack, W. and Levant, R., **New Psychotherapy For Men** (New York, John Wiley and Sons, 1998) chapter 2

25. Ibid., p. 37

26. Ibid., p.36

27. Ibid.

28. Ibid., p. 36

29. Ibid., p. 37

30. Ibid.

31. Ibid., p. 38

32. Ibid., p. 37

33. Ibid., p. 39 & 41

34. Selman, R., **The Growth Of Interpersonal Understanding: Developmental And Clinical Analyses** (New York, Academic Press, 1980)

35. Op. cit., Pollack & Levant, 1998, p. 41

36. Ibid.

37. Op. cit., Gilmore, p. 230

38. West, P., **Conspicuous Compassion: Why Sometimes It Really Is Cruel To Be Kind** (London, CIVITAS, 2004)

39. Nadeau, R., **S/He Brain: Science, Sexual Politics, And The Myths of Feminism** (London, Praeger, 1996) chapter 1

40. Shay, J. and Maltas, C., *in* Pollack, W. and Levant, R., **New Psychotherapy For Men** (New York, John Wiley and Sons, 1998) p. 101

41. Brooks, G., **Gender Sensitive Family Therapy In A Violent Culture** *Family Psychology And Counselling* 1, p. 24-26

42. Pleck, J., **The Gender Role Strain Paradigm: An Update** *in* Levant, R. and Pollack, W., (eds.), **A New Psychology Of Men** (New York, Basic Books, 1995)

43. Op. cit., Pollack & Levant, 1998, p. 43 & 44

44. Ibid., p. 43

45. Ibid.

46. Levant, R. and Kelly, J., **Between Father And Child** (New York, Viking, 1989)

47. Shimanoff, S., **The Role Of Gender In Linguistic References To Emotive States** *Communication Quarterly,* 1983, 31, pp. 174-179

48. Dosser, D., Balswick, J., Halveston, D., **Situational Content Of Emotional Expressions** *Journal of Counselling Psychology*, 1983, 30, pp. 375-387

49. Kelly, H., Cunningham, J., Grisham, J., Lefebvre, H., Sink, C., Yablon, G., **Sex Differences Made During Conflict Within Heterosexual Pairs** *Sex Roles*, 1978, 4, pp. 473-492

50. Op. cit., Dosser et al., 1983

51. Op. cit., Pollack & Levant, 1998, p. 102 & 103

5

Men and Violence

Violence is endemic in our society and in our world. And there is no getting away from the fact that violence is mostly associated with men. No less can we deny that whatever views individuals may hold about the use of violence, society (including women and men), for its own survival and continuing prosperity, demands that certain institutions and roles (occupied largely by males) exercise violence. Those individuals who are called upon to employ means that consequent violence do so with impunity, so long as they act in a manner prescribed and endorsed by society (such as by law or rules of engagement). Concern ourselves as we should with aspirations of how we might like the world to be, we must nonetheless contend with the present realities of biology, society and culture, at whose behest:

> *Men are compelled by moral codes and norms, through psychological and material reward and punishment, to conduct their role principally to ensure the replication of society's primary structures, to defend against, "entropy, human enemies, the forces of nature, time, and all human weaknesses that endanger group life".*[1/2]

Reinforcing masculine biological potentials, manhood ideals appear to be culturally constructed and imposed not as 'mystifications of power relationships', or 'masks for the oppression of women' (as gender feminists suppose), but to benefit and serve the 'collective' and perceived best interests of society – women and men.[3]

FACTORS ASSOCIATED WITH VIOLENCE

What then of the incidence of violence that society does not officially require or condone, which causes much suffering and is predominantly *used by males against males*? Firstly, let us be clear that, whatever the prevalence or problem of violence in our society, *the majority of men are not violent.* And, as we have already noted, violence initiated by women in intimate/partner relationships is at least equal to that of men (a phenomenon that runs contrary to the glib notion that all violence emanates from male constructions of masculinity). The male brain does appear to be tuned for potential aggression (evident in the effects of male hormones acting upon a predisposed male brain). Aggressive, competitive and dominant behaviours have, throughout human history, been genetically rewarded – ensuring their place as an inherent prerogative of the male genetic heritage.[4] However, biology alone cannot account for male violence, because we know that other factors are also associated with violence, such as social and economic conditions, early childhood trauma and abuse, problems of transition (the absence of appropriate male role modelling, rites of passage, and supportive mature male environments), and the use of substances – particularly alcohol.

Socio-economic Environment

There is little doubt that poor, 'dog-eat-dog' environments, in which people must contend with unemployment, boredom, hopelessness, despair, and great competition for few resources, and where the struggle to survive is itself a violating experience, are often environments that breed violence. Such environments exist within and alongside (and invariably impinge upon) affluent ones in all Western societies – including in Australia. Marginalised and neglected, they almost invariably exhibit the recurrent tragedy of normative and generational violence.

Childhood Abuse

Early childhood trauma and abuse is also well known to significantly correlate with later adolescent and adult violence. Though the majority of men who as children suffered abuse and trauma do not use violence against other people, the majority of those that do were abused as children.[5]

The experience of highly intense emotional states of fear and terror, shame, helplessness and rage are common for boys who have been abused. With the exception of rage, such emotions tend to be at odds with the kind of characteristics (such as strength, stoicism, independence and toughness) most commonly emphasised to young males – and which young males are actively internalising. If a boy chooses (as is most likely) to adhere to these characteristics, he must use all his determination to cover over, contain and deny his vulnerability, and dissociate from the bulk of his emotional experience. In this, his pain may become a 'marker of shame, of femininity, of weakness'.[6] Being concerned to conform with manly characteristics, he may be very harsh toward any such signs of 'weakness' or vulnerability in himself or others.[7]

Boyhood abuse, then, can cause a 'potentially toxic amplification' of the demands of the manhood ideal, so that the interaction of the two results in an excessively rigid masculine stance, emotional constriction, and little or no empathy – characteristics commonly exhibited by men who commit violence.[8]

Problems of Transition

A further factor associated with violence – and one that is arguably the most telling in the whole process of male development and maturation – is that of problematic transition: the inability to move successfully from boyhood to mature manhood. The absence or unavailability of appropriate male role modelling, rights of passage, and supportive mature male environments, combined with the confused and often contradictory messages and demands of a male-denigrating culture, has created huge problems for young males in their crucial endeavour to establish a workable sense of masculine adult self-identity.

As a society we appear to be content to allow the situation to exist in which boys must somehow, unassisted, find the means to initiate themselves into mature adulthood. Violence (amongst other inappropriate and harmful behaviours) is all too frequently the consequence of this folly. Violence is commonly associated with ineffectual and self-defeating attempts at self-initiation; it often disguises a desperate though misguided bid to prove oneself worthy of inclusion in the adult world of men. Where growing up (attaining to mature male adulthood) is not achieved, despite reaching the age of adult responsibility, violence may remain as part of a male's behavioural repertoire, and may continue to be used to demonstrate 'manly' credentials. Should we be surprised that we have managed to produce such a large number of impulsive uninitiated pseudo-warriors?

Males caught up in 'boy psychology' lack the understanding that *warrior* (of a kind that is honourable and pro-social) is diminished and invalidated to the degree to which it is not in balance and integrated with other essential masculine/manly attributes, such as compassion, honour, nobility, justice, respectfulness, and a capacity for deep feeling, awe, wonder, sensuality, and being nurturing. 'Man psychology' instead demands the initiated orientation of mind and will, coupled with the earnest commitment and endeavour to realise such attributes in concrete actions, and to give them a differing degree of emphasis and priority, appropriate to particular circumstances.

Males caught up in boy psychology typically confuse impetuosity with heroism and bravery, foolhardiness with courage, selfish lust with love, weakness with sensitivity, dogmatism with discipline; they may wrongly use violence and destruction, not as reluctant actions of last resort or necessity, but for their own sake – to achieve a sense of personal power and causative agency.

Misuse of Alcohol

There are strong statistical relationships between alcohol consumption and crimes of violence in nearly all western countries.[9] Evidence suggests that young males are especially likely to engage in violence after drinking.[10] One study has found that 91% of assaults occurring in public places between 10 a.m. and 2 p.m. were associated with licensed drinking premises.[11]

In the United Kingdom it has been found that in many young populations there is a disturbing relationship between binge drinking and death from violence, both accidental and intentional.[12] Scandinavian research indicates that a 1 litre change in per capita alcohol consumption was associated with a 2 – 10% change in violent criminality.[13]

Much evidence now exists to suggest that alcohol is not only often associated with violence but in fact has a direct causal relationship with violence. New Zealand researchers have argued a direct cause and effect association between adolescent alcohol misuse and heightened risk of violent offending.[14] Research from North America indicates that the evidence for a causal relationship is strong in relation to physical and sexual assaults and for homicide, but is not so clear in relation to domestic violence.[15] In fact, a report from the proceedings of the National Symposium on Alcohol

Misuse and Violence concluded that alcohol was only associated with some instances of domestic violence and not in a causal way. The report further argued, given that violence sometimes occurred when alcohol had not been consumed, did not always occur when alcohol had been consumed – and was sometimes actually less likely to occur when small amounts were consumed, a causal role could not be attributed.[16]

That a strict causal role could not be attributed does not mean that a contributory causal role was eliminated. However, what is observed here of alcohol and domestic violence needs to be viewed in the light of (or considered in relation to) the anomaly already noted: that though males at every age and in every setting appear to be more violent than females, in the context of intimate/partner relationships, male violence is matched or exceeded by that of females.[17]

Another research group has found that alcohol related assaults by female partners are more likely when both partners are heavy drinkers:

> *Typical consumption levels of wives were the only significant predictors of husbands' alcohol-related assaults on wives... Drinking related assaults by wives against husbands were also predictable from women's own consumption patterns and from their aggressive alcohol expectancies.*[18]

However, this was demonstrated using logistic regression analyses, which need to be interpreted with caution.

Factors in Alcohol – Related Violence

Alcohol coupled with preinitiated male posturing is a notoriously bad combination. Feeling stronger and more powerful (the result of inebriation), young males are much more likely to take foolish risks and initiate or participate in violence that might otherwise be avoided, often under the alcohol induced illusion that such behaviour is manly.[19]

Alcohol is a disinhibiting and popular social 'lubricant'. However, associated with young males, it commonly leads to disorderly conduct and violence. Altering human brain functions, it diminishes certain cues normally available as a means of making sense of situations. It also impairs normal personal coping mechanisms, and may exaggerate the perceived threat posed by male competitors.[20]

Some research suggests that where impulsiveness has perhaps presented an obstacle to learning in the early years of male development, a legacy of poor problem-solving may later contribute to aggression. Heavy drinking may serve as an attempt to sublimate or compensate for difficulty with social problem-solving and a limited capacity for social interactions, whilst in effect diminishing their effectiveness – especially amongst other intoxicated male competitors.[21]

It has been a popular view that men's consumption of alcohol has much to do with the conditions they experience in the workforce. However, though this may be true in certain circumstances, research findings about this relationship are contradictory.[22] What can be said is that:

- Across history and cultures, men have consumed more alcohol than women and have caused more problems as a result.[23]

- In cultures where manliness (characterised by toughness and stoicism) is most emphasised, male compared with female alcohol consumption appears to be greater.[24]

- Drinking has often served as a masculinity test, and has been associated with stamina and a preparedness to take risks.[25]

- Drinking in all-male settings has often been a way for men to escape 'control by others, ignore social differences, gain social support, and form strong personal ties with one another'.[26]

- Persistent differences in the way in which men and women use alcohol may be partly attributable to apparent biological differences in how alcohol is absorbed, distributed and metabolised.[27]

- Alcohol consumption may also create a male domain from which women are excluded, because they are unable to compete with men in consumption, and are socially discouraged from doing so.[28]

- Men and women are allowed or encouraged to drink, and to behave when drinking, in different ways. This helps to:

  > ...define and symbolise the social structural distinction between being a man and being a woman.[29]

Whatever the reasons why young males in particular misuse alcohol and sometimes behave antisocially and violently, a good part of the solution to this problem is surely the crucial need for mature male role modelling, and male environments in which progression into mature and responsible male behaviour is both encouraged and demonstrated.

It is ironical that the men most lauded and exalted as 'heroes' and 'icons' of admiration in our society (usually sportsmen), are all too often those who achieve notoriety in their private lives for drunk, disorderly, antisocial and violent behaviour.

A final point to ponder is that in Australia between 1860 and 1901 – despite a growing population – the consumption of alcohol actually fell, which evidence suggests was attributable to the natural processes associated with the growth of cities and urbanisation. Temperance and other prohibitionist movements appear to have had a minimal effect on this trend:

> *When men and women found a variety of alternatives such as home building, involvement in sporting activities and community pastimes, then drinking decreased. Such changes in habits, or more positively, the adoption of worthwhile living practices, came about virtually independent of imposed restrictions.*[30]

Factors Associated With Violence

The majority of men are not violent. Violence is predominantly used by males against males. Violence initiated by women in intimate/partner relationships is at least equal to that of men; in relation to children it exceeds that of men. The incidence of violence of a kind *not* condoned or required by society (of certain institutions and roles) is associated with a range of factors, which include:

Physiology
The Male brain does appear to be tuned for potential aggression evident in the effects of male hormones acting upon a predisposed male brain. Male behaviours (such as aggression, dominance, and competitiveness) have throughout history been genetically rewarded - ensuring their place as an inherent prerogative of the male genetic heritage.

Socio-economic Environment
Poor communities with unemployment, boredom, hopelessness, despair, and where the struggle to survive is itself a violating experience, commonly breed violence.

Childhood Abuse
Though the majority of men who as children suffered abuse and trauma do not use violence against other people, the majority of those who do were abused as children. Boyhood abuse can cause a 'potentially toxic amplification' of the demands of the manhood ideal, so that the interaction of the two results in an excessively rigid masculine stance, emotional constriction, and

---

little or no empathy – characteristics commonly exhibited by men who commit violence.

Problems of Transition
As a society, we appear to be content to allow the situation to exist in which boys must somehow, unassisted, find the means to initiate themselves into mature male adulthood.
Violence is commonly associated with ineffectual and self-defeating attempts at self-initiation.
Where 'growing up' or attaining to mature male adulthood is not achieved, despite reaching the age of adult responsibility, violence may remain as part of a male's behavioural repertoire, and may continue to be used to demonstrate 'manly' credentials.

Misuse of Alcohol
Much evidence now exists to suggest that alcohol is not only often associated with violence but in fact has a direct causal relationship with violence. Such evidence appears strong in relation to physical and sexual assaults and for homicide, but is not so clear in relation to domestic violence; alcohol is only associated with some instances of domestic violence and may not be a causal factor.

Alcohol coupled with preinitiated male posturing is a notoriously bad combination. It alters human brain functions, diminishes cues normally available as a means of making sense of situations, impairs normal coping mechanisms, and may exaggerate the perceived threat posed by male competitors.

Drinking has often served as a masculinity test; where manliness (characterised by toughness and stoicism) is most emphasised, male compared to female alcohol consumption tends to be greater.

Alcohol consumption may also importantly create a male domain from which women are excluded, because they are unable to compete with men in consumption, and are socially discouraged from doing so.

Much of the solution to the problem of alcohol-related violence comes back to the crucial need for mature male role modelling, and male environments in which progression into mature and responsible male behaviour is both encouraged and demonstrated.

Table 9

References

1.	Ashfield, J., **Gender, Masculinity and Manhood: Core Concepts For Understanding Men's Issues** (Western Australia, Ikon Publications, 2003), page. 49 *This Book has been revised and reissued under the title: The Making Of A Man: Reclaiming masculinity and manhood in the light of reason (South Australia, Peacock Publications, 2004)*

2.	Gilmore, D., **Manhood In the Making** (U.S.A Yale University Press, 1990) p. 226

3.	Op. cit., Ashfield, p. 49

4.	Daly, M. and Wilson, M., **Competitiveness, Risk- taking And Violence: The Young Male Syndrome** *Ethology And Sociobiology,* 1985, pp. 6, 59-73

5.	Lisak, D., Hopper, J., Song, P., **Factors In The Cycle Of Violence: Gender Rigidity And Emotional Constriction** *Journal of Traumatic Stress,* 1996, p. 721-743

6.	Lisak, D., **Confronting and Treating Empathic Disconnection In Violent Men** *in* Pollack, W. and Levant, R., **New Psychotherapy For Men** (U.S.A., John Wiley and Sons, 1998) pp. 219-220

7.	Ibid., pp. 219-220

8.	Ibid.

9.	**Alcohol and Violence – What's the Connection** (New Zealand, Alcohol and Public Health Research Unit, archived 30/06/2002) Available online – www.aphru.ac.nz/hot/violence.htm.

10.	Homel, R., Tomsen, R., Tommeny, J., **Public Drinking and Violence: Not Just an Alcohol Problem** *The Journal Of Drug Issues,* 1992, pp. 22(3), 679-697

11. Ireland, C. and Tommeny, J., **The Crime Cocktail: Licenced Premises, Alcohol and Street Offences** *Drug and Alcohol Review*, 1993, pp. 12, 7, 143-150

12. Op. cit., **Alcohol and Violence – What's The Connection**

13. Ibid.

14. Ibid.

15. **10th Special Report to the U.S Congress on Alcohol and Health from the Secretary of Health and Human Services, National Institute of Health, National Institute on Alcohol Abuse and Alcoholism** (United States Department of Health and Human Services, 2000)

16. Wallace, A., Edgar, S., Howard, J., Fiswick, E., Roberts, G., Klein, L., McMilan, L., Drake, R., **Violence Against Women And Children In the Home** *Proceedings of the National Symposium On Alcohol Misuse and Violence, Report 4* (Australian Government Publishing Service, Canberra, 1994)

17. Moffit, T., Caspi, A., Rutter, M., Silva, P., **Sex Differences In Antisocial Behaviour: Conduct Disorder, Delinquency, and Violence In the Dunedin Longtitudinal Study** (U.K, Cambridge University Press, 2001)

18. Kaumen Kantor, G. and Asoligian, N., **Gender Differences In Alcohol-Related Spousal Aggression** *in* Wilsnack, R. and Wilsnack, S., (eds.) **Gender And Alcohol: Individual And Social Perspectives** (New Brunswick, U.S.A., Rutgers Center of Alcohol Studies, 1997) pp. 312-334

19. Op.cit., **Alcohol And Violence – What's The Connection?**

20. Ibid.

21. McMurran, M., Blair, M., Egan, V., **An Investigation Of The Correlations Between Aggression, Impulsiveness, Social Problem-solving, And Alcohol Use** *Aggressive Behaviour*, vol 26 (6) (U.S.A., Wiley-Liss, 2002) pp. 439-445

22. Blum, T. and Roman, P., **Employment And Drinking** *in* Wilsnack, R. and Wilsnack S., (eds.) **Gender And Alcohol: Individual And Social Perspectives** (U.S.A. Rutgers Centre of Alcohol Studies, 1997) pp. 312-334

23. Wilsnack, R. and Wilsnack, S., (eds.) **Gender and Alcohol Individual And Social Perspectives** (U.S.A., Rutgers Center of Alcohol Studies, 1997) Introduction

24. McDonald, M., (ed.) **Gender, Drink And Drugs** (Providence, U.S.A., Berg Pub., 1994)

25. McDonald, M., **Drinking And Social Identity In The West of France** *in* Macdonald, M., (ed.) **Gender Drink And Drugs** (Providence, U.S.A., Berg Pub., 1994) pp. 99-124

26. Op. cit., Wilsnack & Wilsnack, Introduction

27. Ibid.

28. Op. cit., McDonald, 1994

29. Op. cit., Wilsnack & Wilsnack, Introduction

30. Powell, K., **Drinking and Alcohol In Colonial Australia, 1788-1901 For the Eastern Colonies** *Monograph Series.* (Canberra, Australian Government Publishing Service, 1988)

Part Two

Affirming Masculinity and Enhancing Manhood

Prologue

In Part 1 it was argued that manhood (which is rooted in and inseparable from male physiology) is essential both to human survival and the stability, security, and quality of life we have come to expect and demand. The manhood ideal to which men are compelled to conform (whether or not they find it psychologically congenial), though varying in emphasis at different times and in different circumstances of societal need, has an indispensable role and inevitable continuity.

It was also noted that inadequacies of current male role socialisation, and a scarcity of supportive and exemplary mature male environments, result inpotential difficulties of early male psychological and character development, and a manhood ideal lacking important elements conducive to masculine maturity and moral integrity. Whilst such problems warrant urgent attention, any attempt at remedy only has legitimacy within a framework that is congruent and not at odds with the irreducible reality of masculinity and the social necessity of manhood. Any denigration of maleness by attempting to coerce boys or men into mimicking female/feminine ways of being or behaving, is misguided and has the potential to be damaging and dehumanising.

The appropriate socialisation, psychological and moral development of boys, and the attainment of mature manhood by both boys and men, are only possible based on the full repertoire of manly attributes associated with a mature manhood (characterised by mature adult rather than immature adolescent psychology).

The prevailing manhood ideal will more properly deserve to be called an *ideal*, only when the neglected and undervalued masculine attributes (and the essential balance they contribute) are reinstated and accorded the role and honour they deserve. Such attributes are termed here *masculine attributes*, because how they are configured and 'inspirited' within the masculine psyche, and how and with what energy they are borne out in men's actions, will be most often uniquely masculine.

Only out of the wholeness of this properly constituted masculine ideal can boys be appropriately socialised; only in honest pursuit of this ideal can men lay claim to true manliness. And we are not just talking here about grasping or pursuing an idea. Nobility is not just an inspiring or nice idea, nor is it a birthright; it is something borne out in one's actions. The worth of any ideal should become evident in the marketplace of life.

We must go further still than to propose a reconstituted manhood ideal, and also explore by what means boys and men can be launched or initiated into this ideal and the pursuit of it, in the absence of socially authorised and validated rights of passage.

This work with men and boys is urgently needed in order to decisively supplant the disastrous prevailing tendency in our culture to devalue and demean the masculinity of boys and men.

6

Reconstituting the Manhood Ideal

Today, as in any generation, there is no more important issue or urgent need than that of the formation of human character.* Despite our technological sophistication and affluent modernity, we are no less susceptible to the dehumanising excesses, self-centredness and moral corruption exhibited by previous generations. We struggle as did they with the difficulty of keeping goodness connected with power; with the pursuit of material prosperity in balance with what is truly in the best interests of human society. Though these are issues of general human character – of men and women, here we must concern ourselves with the particular institution of manhood and the character and calibre of men.

The most emphasised and conspicuous features of manhood today (which are the basis of male role socialisation), appear to reflect our current aggressive societal pursuit of 'the biggest piece of the world's pie' that can be had. 'Cut-throat' competitiveness and a 'hard-nosed' 'elbowing one's way to the front of the line' appear to

---

* Character defined as: the inherent complex of attributes that determine a person's moral and ethical actions and reactions.

characterise our social, economic and political institutions. But is this orientation (and the orientation of manhood it requires) serving to enhance our quality of life? Perhaps in some respects it does. But in what significant ways might it also be diminishing us? Have we lost a necessary sense of balance and perspective; are we losing touch with sensual and aesthetic humanness, the meaning, moral imagination and nobility that render culture rich, vibrant and progressive (the stuff of civilisation)? Have we become nonchalant about character?

The societal neglect of character and virtue, of values and moral consciousness – in deference to cynical materialism, a consumptive mentality and the paranoia of protectionism these consequent – creates dangerous deficiencies not only in the way manhood is constituted (because of what is demanded of it), but as well in culture. It gives rise to a 'vacancy' in culture, one happily (though unfortunately) occupied by 'pop-star squatters, trumped-up magnificoes... (and) tinsel celebrites'.[1] These become the malnourishing role models to which young people aspire. Though the mass media reports some examples of exemplary human character and accomplishment, because of their paucity they tend to seem somewhat exotic and unusually and unattainably heroic.

Boys becoming adult in age, and men in general, need (and have always needed) to distinguish and prove themselves in some way. However, without adequate emphasis on character as integral to this endeavour, and on achievement measured against attributes of mature masculinity, they may well distinguish themselves not in nobility or virtue but in ways that are an offence to manhood, with consequent harm to themselves and others.

It is important to reiterate: there is virtue in masculine strength, self-reliance, self-denial, aggressive drive, unyielding determination and industry, self-sacrificing protectiveness, a capacity to strictly regulate thoughts and emotions, and even in sexual appetite, but only integrated with other counterbalancing, complementary and humanising attributes. Such attributes are essential to a properly constituted manhood ideal – an ideal conducive to and productive of masculine maturity and moral integrity. Only such an ideal can remedy the current inadequacies in male role socialisation, and provide a profile of mature masculinity, a basis for psychological well-being, and the threshold and pathway for boys' and men's quest for honourable manhood.

Reinstating the neglected masculine attributes may be understood as involving two major tasks: firstly, naming, expounding, and recognising the enduring nature and efficacy of these attributes; secondly, identifying and promoting the means by which boys aspiring to manhood, and men, can be inspired and enlisted by them, and experience being launched or initiated into a commitment to and pursuit of them. What is proposed in this and the following chapter is intended to assist anyone interested in better understanding and/or participating in this endeavour.

'BOY PSYCHOLOGY' VERSUS 'MAN PSYCHOLOGY'

A useful starting point for compiling a profile of the kind of attributes previously referred to, is to contrast and compare what has been termed 'boy psychology' (considered, 'skewed, stunted and false') with 'man psychology', characterised by compassion, generativity, wisdom and moral integrity.[2]

Unlike boy psychology, man psychology reflects moral character, self-insight and maturity; it exhibits certain moral attributes: rather than being self-absorbed (which is self-defeating) and indifferent to others, it is self-respectful and prosocial – respectful of others. Such attributes, in proper relation to other elements of the manhood ideal, humanise, 'consciencise' and 'sanctify' them – rendering manhood and masculinity honourable.

An analogy can be drawn from the transformation of power said to have occurred within the incomparably wealthy Rothschild family, whose immense power of wealth consequented some infamously cruel injustices – until a new generation of sons awakened to the need for power to be joined with goodness. They turned the vast family fortune over to numerous philanthropic endeavours – with the effect of restoring moral integrity and honour to the family.

The catalogue of dispositions and behaviours (opposite), though of course not comprehensive, serves to highlight what may be considered mature manliness, and the kind of transformations that initiation might be expected to commence (which will be discussed at length in a subsequent chapter).

Boy Psychology	*Man Psychology*
Dismisses and avoids most emotion except anger.	Is deep feeling; acknowledges, is responsible for, and works with emotions and experience, using reflection, solitude, and action/ritual.
Feels awkward with and shrinks from tenderness and gentleness.	Values and welcomes tenderness and gentleness, and knows when, where, and how to receive, exhibit and verbalise them.
Feels the need to appear tough and in control at all times.	Is discerning and thoughtful in using strength and reflecting strength. Chooses to be vulnerable in appropriate circumstances.
Tends to be moody, reactive sulky and uncommunicative.	Endeavours to identify and work on issues that influence mood, and keeps communication open, civil and constructive.
Is given to volatility and outbursts of anger or rage.	Recognises the early signs of feeling powerless, 'cornered', 'hedged in' or angry. Harnesses anger for self-insight and problem solving, by delaying action until 'grounded' in good sense and constructive-ness.
Is ashamed of and covers over (or aggressively acts out) feelings of fear, vulnerability and insecurity.	Is not ashamed of fear, vulnerability and insecurity; endeavours to make an opportunity and find an environment in which these feelings can be safely acknowledged, perhaps verbalised, and worked through, avoiding their merging into anger, and their expression in aggression. Knows when and in which circumstances it is appro-priate both to suppress and if need be reconnect with such experience.

Takes foolish and dangerous risks.	Takes dangerous risks only when it is crucial to do so. Uses thoughtful and courageous risk-taking to overcome personal fears, achieve manly character, and to protect others.
Is unforgiving, vengeful, and a 'sore loser'.	Can both accept and extend forgiveness. Seeks justice not vengeance. Uses the disappointment of losing constructively.
Shows contempt for other people's weakness, fear and vulnerability.	Is aware of the tendency to project self-contempt onto others. Seeks to empathise with other's weakness, fear and vulnerability, acting compassion-ately, sometimes firmly, and without condescension.
Exhibits little self-insight or self-awareness.	Actively cultivates self-insight and self-awareness as vital keys to personality and character development.
Over emphasises and over-burdens sex as a means of meeting sexual intimacy needs.	Values sexual interest, experience, and appetite; does not diminish sex by expecting of it the satisfaction of emotional need that cannot be fully met by it, but only with other means of emotional nurture.
Tends to fear and feel overpowered by women and mature men.	Is not vulnerable to feeling overpowered by the feminine or the authentically masculine, because it is not emotionally dependent (or vulnerable), and it knows the mature masculine to be supportive and respectful, and never overpowering or exploitative.
Is emotionally dependent on women; is reliant on them for emotional nurture, balance, stability and a sense of wellbeing.	Acknowledges and values the feminine emotion faculty with its nurturing and humanising qualities, but does not relinquish

responsibility for emotional wellness and stability to women or female partners.

Accepts responsibility for its own emotional health, equilibrium and nurture, whilst also benefiting from women's important emotional contribution to relationship. Is able to bring to relationships emotional qualities and benefits of a uniquely masculine nature.

Is intolerant to criticism.

Sifts and processes criticism thoughtfully, utilising it or, if appropriate, dissociating from it.

May be addictively obsessed with pleasure and experience; always restless, impulsive, living for the moment through parties, travel, food, drugs, sex and/or high levels of arousal; caught up in an endless cycle of highs and lows, pleasure and pain; lost in an 'ocean of the senses' but never really experiencing subtleties, only gross sensations; ever living on the periphery of self.

Is deep feeling and deeply sensual, alert to and able to savour and appreciate colour, texture, form and beauty. Is vividly alive and passionate, yet grounded, centred, calm, integrated, and 'body inhabiting' – that is, tuned in to and respectful of body sensations. Lives out of a stable and acknowledged self, and has the sensitivity and vitality to fully experience pleasure and promote pleasure in others, without falling into 'idolatry'.

Uses people, and values material things.

Values self and others, and sees material things as means not ends in the pursuit of quality of life.

Is narcissistic, self-absorbed and self-serving.

Has a healthy sense of self-worth and self-efficacy, and is able to (and inclined to) value and respect others.

Has little sense of justice except when itself is wronged, and has little sensitivity or concern for the needs or rights of others.

Has a passionate and deep sense of justice, and a sensitivity and empathy for those who are oppressed, downtrodden or wronged. Translates concern into appropriate actions.

Is easily crushed by the humiliation, guilt or disappointment of failure, and succumbs to despair, self-directed violence, or mental paralysis.	Is pained and even 'struck down' by failure and the experience of guilt, but decides not to indulge paralysis, and sets about to make things right. Makes a new beginning, informed by the lessons of failure; recognises that a foolish or cowardly act doesn't make a foolish or cowardly man.
Is jealous of others' success and envious of others' wealth.	Learns from others' success. Can discern the difference between authentic and illusory success, and affirms that each individual's gifts, talents and life's purpose are different. Recognises that real success results from authenticity – being true to one's own self and 'calling' within the freedom and with the resources available. Is aware that whatever wealth is possible or appropriate for an individual, it will likely not be achieved without hard work and perseverance.
Will cheat on a partner.	Confronts the difficulties in a relationship and, if need be, sets about the task and works through the grief of ending it, before becoming intimate with a new partner.
Abuses alcohol or other substances.	Doesn't try to extinguish or sublimate existential or emotional pain with substances, but acknowledges emotion and experience, and works with them with patience and determination. Finds a way forward, however difficult – including by enlisting the expertise and support of others. Uses alcohol sensibly and responsibly

Does not accept responsibility, whether for feelings, behaviour, health or self-care.	Accepts responsibility for own feelings and behaviour. Does not play 'victim' to avoid effort and responsibility. Acknowledges that some situations (as part of a man's role) may compromise health and wellbeing, but in all other circumstances mature men take care of their physical and mental health.
Blames parents and/or others for misfortune, emotional or psychological state, or personality.	Recognises that whatever is past cannot be changed, and though present circumstances and experience appear intractable, what remains is the freedom to choose one's attitude in these circumstances, and ways of constructively tackling the challenge of changing one's mental state and life for the better. Recognises that bemoaning the past or present changes nothing, and that mental health (and the capacity to make something of one's life) is based on a degree of tension, – 'the tension between what one is and what one should become'.[3]
Hero-worships – relinquishing responsibility to a hero (or hero figure) for acting humanely, courageously, heroically or with moral integrity.	Respects and seeks to emulate the qualities of noble men. Recognises that the honourable things about exemplary men are not their sole prerogative but the heritage of all men – the potential in them awaiting realisation. Never leaves it to others alone to act with character, but joins with them in the tradition of endeavouring to do what men of good will have always done.
Wastes money on childish pursuits, shifting from one fad or novelty to another.	Has aspirations, goals, clarified purpose and priorities, which are the appropriate focus for

	available resources. Considers own and others' needs thoughtfully and fairly. Does not overlook the need for enjoyment, pleasure, fun or spontaneity, but these are interwoven with, and do not take priority over, the pursuit of aspirations and goals.
Uses power for self-advancement and self-aggrandisement.	Uses power cautiously, thoughtfully and morally. Views power as a means to moral ends, and its accumulation as always needing to be commensurate with a just and morally legitimate purpose. Recognises that the use of power to benefit self or others apart from these criteria becomes abusive, unjust and corruptive.
Uses violence to achieve; a sense of personal power, causative agency and self-aggrandisement.	Views violence as a reluctant, thoughtful, carefully measured action of last resort. Considers war, human suffering, and destruction as repugnant. Achieves a sense of personal efficacy, dignity, meaning, purpose and causative agency by being creative, generative and morally purposive.
Takes more than it gives in relationships.	Though making a masculine not feminine contribution to relationship, recognises relationship, relatedness, and interdependence as the core essence of reality. Realises that men must nurture and invest in their relationships beyond what they may need to draw from them.
Practises 'trophy sex' (or 'scoring') and uses women.	Treats women honestly, respectfully – never exploitatively. Negotiates the meaning and responsibilities of sexual intimacy. Fully enjoys sex but not at another's expense. Seeks authentic, self-developing and pro-social ways of distinguishing itself.

Lacks a sense of meaningful connection with the natural environment; is prone to abusing, neglecting, and destructively exploiting it.

Has a deep respect for and sense of connectedness with the environment. Acknowledges and accepts responsibility for its stewardship, reasonable protection and care. Values its beauty, its moods, seasons, and transformative power for the human psyche. Gives it due regard as the sustaining basis of all life.

Fears and hits out against difference and things it doesn't understand – such as ethnicity, gender and religious differences.

Does not idealise either sameness or difference but values both. Is engaged in the endeavour to achieve human understanding, respect, unity and justice in diversity. Seeks to appreciate and be enriched by difference, without succumbing to self- diminishing cultural deca- dence. Overcomes fear and misunderstanding through active dialogue, respectful enquiry, intelligent analysis, empathy, and compassion.

Is dismissive of and unconcerned with all but mechanical/material reality – or what can be seen, measured, analysed, bought, sold, consumed or possessed.

Has a capacity for deep feeling, awe and wonder. Has a sense of, feels drawn to, and desires to somehow know, experience and achieve a more conscious relationship with the unseen greater reality, to which mythology and spiritual traditions attest.

Though focussed on self, is unable to act effectively or creatively for itself, and has little positive impact on, nor makes a contribution to others.

Is creative, generative, and giving; it vivifies and makes alive itself and others. Its plenty in some way encourages, nurtures, motivates or sustains others.

Exhibits little capacity for self-discipline, determination or perseverance.

Cultivates self-discipline to achieve freedom from disorder, dispersion and the depressing inertia of failing to accomplish meaningful goals. Fosters a degree of self-discipline that can encompass, balance, and ensure due regard for psychological, physical, spiritual and social needs.

Fears and avoids authenticity, because it demands the courage of conviction, self-responsibility, vulnerability and self-discipline.	Strives for authenticity through which to achieve unique personality, life direction, purpose and meaning. Contends with vulnerability, fear and the misunderstanding of others by ensuring that choices and actions are congruent with and informed by sound values – values that require consideration of others but not compliance with their demands.
Avoids things serious: is intellectually lazy, dogmatic, inflexible, thinks only concretely and simplis-tically.	Endeavours to consider and reflect on a wide variety of issues; thinks broadly, sifts and compares ideas and is open to new knowledge – open to change. Values, honours, and seeks to acquire wisdom.
Uses knowledge to manipulate and control others to achieve a sense of superiority or self-elevation.	Recognises that knowledge is power and must be used with moral integrity and generosity; it should not be withheld from others in order to control them or manipulate them for selfish gain. Uses knowledge for the genuine betterment and benefit of self and others.
Is rigidly proud, egocentric and unyielding.	Exhibits strength and courage in humility. Can readily admit wrong and apologise. Shows fortitude in matters of principle and importance, yet coupled with compassion, mercy and goodness.
Is impetuous, foolhardy and given to posturing.	Exhibits courage and bravery in thoughtful and needful behaviours. Has no need of boasting or posturing, because it does not suffer from an ailing ego,

but instead is ordered, integrated, and has a strong sense of purposeful direction. It has nothing to prove except fidelity to its own destiny and calling. Within and through this dynamic order, spontaneity, creativity and manly wildness are readily expressed.

Is aggressively competitive in all circumstances

Is strongly competitive when necessary and appropriate. Is equally adept in the use of co-operation, and can suspend competitiveness in order to be co-operative wherever it is possible and appropriate to do so.

From this brief catalogue a basic profile of core attributes can be identified – those essential for the moral integrity of the manhood ideal. Such attributes are the wellsprings of manly character attested to by the myths, legends, moral fables and sacred writings which distil the wisdom of the ages. Through these media, these attributes have always resonated within men's hearts, fired their imaginations, and proven able to permeate and transform personality and behaviour; they have provided a basis for moral consciousness, and a moral orientation and underpinning for volition and motives. Such attributes have historically been considered the true marks of human virtue and eminence – the greatness of exemplary men. Such people are:

> ...always used by a culture: to inspire ordinary lives by displaying their own potentialities. Extraordinary people excite; they guide; they warn; standing as they do, in the corridors of imagination – statues of greatness... they help us carry what comes to us as it came to them. That's what we look for when buying biographies and reading the secret intimacies of the famous... Not to pull them down to our level, but to lift ours, making our world less impossible through familiarity with theirs. These personifications of heightened imagination burn right into the soul and are its teachers.[4]

It would appear that these attributes of exemplary manhood are not merely cultural artifacts, but robust potentials of heritable and cultural continuity selected into our psychic constitution and reinforced by culture, because of their crucial importance to group life and survival. Their transcultural recurrence and mythocultural universality supports this idea.[5/6/7/8]

As with other masculine potentials, their realisation depends on a conducive sociocultural environment which endorses, values, amplifies, reinforces, summons and celebrates them.

Attributes of Mature Manhood

Adept with Emotions
Valuing
Managing
Nurturing
Expressing
Understanding
Utilising

Self-disciplined
Ordered
Balanced
Purposeful
Persevering
Goal oriented
Strong
Undaunted
Committed

Risk Taking
Thoughtful
Purposeful
Self-confronting
Courageous
Brave
Self-giving
Protective
Character building

Shows Great Strength
Humility
Forgiveness
Apology
Generosity
Mercy
Goodness

Owns Responsibility
Emotions
Behaviour
Physical health
Mental health
Personal Development
Accomplishment
Seeking purpose
Setting goals
Realising aspirations
Material sufficiency
Resolving difficulties in
relationship
Contributing to relationship
Appropriate communication

Open to Greater Reality
Deep feeling
Reflective
Aesthetic
Capacity for wonder
Capacity for awe
Desire for meaning
Desire to experience, to know,
to be in right relationship with
greater reality
Desire for wholeness and
goodness

**Faithful Steward of the
Natural Environment**
Values
Respects
Protects
Uses thoughtfully and carefully
Knows it is the basis of all life
Knows its transformative
power
Works for its health/wellbeing

Strives for Authenticity
Self-insightful
Self-aware
Self-accepting
Unique Personality
Own life direction
Own purpose
Own aspirations
Own goals
Thoughtful
Considerate of others
Vitally alive
Enlivening of others
Dauntless
Disciplined
Just

Values Difference and Diversity
Ethnic
Cultural
Intellectual
Religious
Spiritual
Gender
Behaviour
Political
Is discerning
Is thoughtful
Is open
Is flexible
Avoids-idealisation
Cultural decadence
Sycophantism
Self-abasement

Champion of Justice
Passionate
Self-confronting
Honest
Decisive
Takes action
Protective
Deep feeling
Empathic concern for the
oppressed, down trodden,
poor, dispossessed, wronged
Peacemaking
Compassionate
Merciful

Masters Adversity
Strong
Ordered
Disciplined
Thoughtful
Constructive
Undaunted by failure
Undaunted by guilt
Undaunted by others'
apparent success
Deep convictions
Perseverance
Commitment
Self-belief

Generative
Creative
Visionary
Imaginative
Hard working
Enlivening
Innovative
Productive
Uplifting
Motivating
Giving
Morally reflective

Deeply Sensual
Aesthetic
Reflective
Mindful
Self-aware
Self-insightful
Sexual
Loving
Respectful
Savours Experience
Aware of body sensations
Deep feeling
Sensitive
Celebratory
Vividly alive
Grounded
'Wild'
Passionate

Morally Noble
Wise
Seeks wisdom
Trustworthy with power
Trustworthy with knowledge
Just
Truthful
Deeply considerate
Scrupulous
Mindful
Thoughtful
Reflective
Consultative
Views abuse of power as
repugnant
Compassionate
Strong
Disciplined

Cultivates the Mind
Values ideas
Values thinking
Seeks knowledge
Seeks wisdom
Expands and develops mind
Values intellectual integrity
Does not just believe but
exercises intelligence

Competitive and Cooperative
Appropriately competitive
Nurtures cooperation
Nurtures collaboration
Nurtures community
Nurtures relationship
Thoughtful
Prosocial
Generous
Principled
Just

Table 10

Essential Attributes for the Manhood Ideal

Adept with Emotions

Risk-taking

Shows Great Strength

Champion of Justice

Deeply sensual

Open to Greater Reality

Values Difference and Diversity

Faithful Steward of the Natural Environment

Self-disciplined

Generative

Masters adversity

Owns responsibility

Morally noble

Cultivates the Mind

Strives for Authenticity

Table 11

Two authors of note who have also endeavoured to set down alternative models of mature manhood are Aaron Kipnis and Sam Keen – both prominent leaders of the North American men's movement (known to Americans as the Mythopoetic Men's Movement).

Kipnis (an academic and Neojungain psychotherapist), in his book *Knights Without Armor*, makes a comparison between a deficient model of manhood, what he terms 'heroic hypermasculinity' with 'feminised hypomasculinity', and 'authentic integrated masculinity'. He is quick to point out that attributes ascribed to feminised men are not meant to describe the attributes of women or homosexual men. He states that:

> *Whereas femininity is a life-affirming force in women, it can represent hypo-masculinity in men. In this form it is just as toxic as the hyper-masculinity of the heroic male.*[9]

	Deficient Versus Mature Masculinity		
	Uninitiated		**Inititiated**
Arena	*Deficient (Hyper)* *Masculinity*	*Feminised (Hypo)* *Masculinity*	*Mature (Integrated) Masculinity*
Physical	Dominating	Submissive	Capable
	Controlling	Controlled	Vigilant
	Tough	Gentle	Strong
	Soldier	Pacifist	Warrior
	Lord/master	Consort	Husband/partner
	Coercive	Pliant	Firm
	Destructive	Immobile	Generative
Emotional	Closed	Unprotected	Receptive
	Numb	Flooded	Feeling
	Co-dependent	Dependent	Interdependent
	Demanding	Smothering	Nurturing
	Aggressive	Passive	Assertive
	Cynical	Naïve	Fresh/Humorous
	Sex partner	Pleaser	Lover
	Defensive	Wounded	Deep Feeling
	Repressed	Contained	Wild/Playful
Mental	Compartmentalised	Merged	Eclectic
	Penetrating	Diffused	Insightful
	Splitting	Joining	Holds paradox
	Linear	Circular	Holonomic
	Hierarchy	Anarchy	Community
	Exploitative	Conservative	Resourceful
	Rules and Laws	Procedures	Personal Ethics
	Pedant	Magical Thinker	Healer
Spiritual	Absolutist	Dualistic	Paradoxical
	Uninitiated	Seeker	Initiated
	Immobile	In flight	Grounded
	Divided	Dissociated	Embodied
	Dogma	Belief	Direct Experience
	Exclusive	Inclusive	Selective
	Priest	Guru	Mentor/elder

Table 12
Excerpt adapted from: Kipnis, A., *Knights Without Armor* (U.S.A., Jeremy P. Archer Inc., 1991) p.99

Sam Keen (a philosopher and author) considers current constructions of masculinity and manliness outmoded, and believes there is a widening gap between the traditional masculine ideal and the 'new quantum, ecological, cooperative worldview'. He proposes a 'sampler of heroic virtues' (of 'modern heroic man'), to which men can aspire; a 'portrait of now and future man at his best'.[10]

The following excerpts reflect the virtues Keen believes should be part of a redefined manhood:

The Virtue of Wonder
It is ancient wisdom that true virility is rooted in wonder. To wonder is to open ourselves to the gift of being. Before we can act with integrity, before we can think with respect, we must pause to wonder.[11]

The Virtue of Empathy
"...spiritual availability"...The unavailable man is encumbered with himself. The available person is not encumbered by his possessions or his self-image, and hence has the capacity to listen and respond to the appeal made by others on him.[12]

The Virtue of a Heartful Mind
We need to acquire a heartful mind. This seems best done through the cultivated discipline of solitude, and the habit of recollection and autobiographical thinking. I must take time to be with myself, to discover my desires, my rhythms, my tastes, my gifts, my hopes, my wounds.[13]

The Virtue of Moral Outrage
...the best men are...spiritual warriors who are alive with moral outrage...if our minds are heartful, we must be outraged by the cruelty in the world, and realise that it is our vocation to become protectors of the powerless

and healers of the broken. To guard against self-righteousness ...I must constantly remind myself that I am part of the problem I am trying to solve, I am also the enemy against whom I must fight...[14]

The Virtue of Right Livelihood
To return the sense of dignity and honour to manhood, we have to stop pretending that we can make a living at something that is trivial or destructive and still have a legitimate self-worth...where many people are condemned to deadening and trivial jobs, it is often necessary to find a way to express vocational gifts apart from work.[15]

The Virtue of Enjoyment
...we will gain the desire and wisdom to create a more compassionate society only when we learn to take our time and find passionate enjoyment in elemental pleasures. We feel outrage, and respond to the vocation to protect against desecration, only when we have previously sensed the deep-down sacredness of our own flesh.[16]

The Virtue of Friendship
We need same-sex friends because there are types of validation and acceptance that we receive only from our gender-mates. There is much about out experience as men that can only be shared with, and understood by, other men. Only men understand the secret fears that go with the territory of masculinity.[17]

The Virtue of Communion
...men's loneliness is a measurement of the degree to which we have ignored the fundamental truth of interdependence. To pretend that a man standing tall and alone is virile is to base our view of manhood on

a metaphysic of separation that has been shown to be an illusion by almost every advance of the physical and social sciences of our era.[18]

The Virtue of Husbanding
As men, our vocation has something to do with being guardians of the future. A husbandman may or may not plow and sow crops, but he certainly must take care of the place with which he has been entrusted. To husband is to practise the art of stewardship, to oversee, to make judicious use of things, and to conserve for the future. Psychologically, the husbandman is a man who has made a decision to be in place, to make commitments, to forge bonds, to put down roots, to translate the feeling of empathy and compassion into an action of caring.[19]

The Virtue of Wildness
Wildness first and foremost comes from our identification with the literal wilderness...Wildness is no metaphor whose meaning we may learn when we are comfortably housed within a city or enclosed within the boundaries of the civilized psyche. We need large expanses of untouched wilderness to remind ourselves of the abiding fundamental truth of the human condition...[20] *After nearly a century of urban living, men's dreams still testify that we belong in the wilderness. We dream of breaking free and escaping to "a men's place" under open sky, a place where physical strength counts and clocks do not dictate the rhythms of the day. Wendall Barry says it best: "Now it is only in the wild places that a man can sense the verity of being a man. In the crowded places he is more and more closed in by the feeling that he is ordinary and that he is, on the average, expendable..."*[21]

THE NEOJUNGIAN VIEW OF ARCHETYPES AND THE MATURE MASCULINE

Previously it was suggested that attributes of exemplary manhood appear to be potentials of heritable and cultural continuity whose realisation (in men's consciousness and behaviour) depends on a conducive sociocultural environment. This view is not incompatible with the contemporary rendition of Carl Jung's work, popular in the writings of the Mythopoetic Men's Movement.

Neojungians believe that the attributes of exemplary manhood are potent and enduring because they originate in what are termed masculine *archetypes*.[22] It was Jung's belief (based on his extensive research) that at the level of the deep unconscious every person's psyche is grounded in and connected with what he called the *collective unconscious.* He suggested that this common layer (connecting all people of all cultures) is a vast repository of ethnic, ancestral and collective memories, containing the entire historical and cultural heritage of mankind's evolution, born anew in the brain structure of every individual'; it is 'the source of the instinctual forces of the psyche and of the forms or categories that regulate them, namely the archetypes'.[23]

Contemporary Jungians affirm that archetypes provide us with a rich and limitless inner resource. There are archetypes that 'pattern the thoughts and feelings and relationships of women, and there are archetypes that pattern the thoughts and feelings and relationships of men'.[24] For men these archetypes are believed to be the source of *masculine potentials* – the basis of a calm and positive mature masculinity. They are thought to be a potential patterning, shaping and organising force within the psyche. They have been likened to a magnet beneath a sheet of paper:

As iron filings are sprinkled over the top of the paper, they immediately arrange themselves into patterns along the lines of magnetic force. We can see the patterns of the filings on the paper, but we can't see the magnet beneath the paper – or, better, we can never see the magnetic force itself, only the visible evidence of its existence. The same is true of archetypes. They remain hidden. But we experience their effects – in art, in poetry, in music, in religion, in our scientific discoveries, in our patterns of behaviour and of thought and feeling. All the products of human creativity and human interaction are like the iron filings. We can see something of the shapes and patterns of the archetypes through these manifestations.[25]

Neojungians would argue that why we don't see more evidence of these archetypes orientating manhood, and consequently influencing male role socialisation and development, is because of a variety of ways in which men have been blocked from experiencing them, including: the disappearance of important ritual processes and ritual elders; a style of modern life that encourages men to live on the psychological periphery of themselves; the unavailability of all-male environments that promote and model what it is to be a mature man; that myth and mythic imagination have been largely eclipsed by pseudo-scientific rationalism and materialism; the prevalence of male-debasing attitudes, messages, institutional policies and practices in our culture. These are all thought to constitute critical contemporary impediments in men's receptivity to archetypal potentials.[26]

Originally, Jung based his view of the collective unconscious and archetypes on clinical evidence from the dreams and daydreams of patients, and on his exhaustive observations and research of the symbols and motifs of mythology and religion from many different parts of the world. Jung recalled the experience of a schizophrenic patient who had a peculiar and elaborate 'vision' with respect to the sun. Jung later came across a translation of an ancient religious manuscript (of Mithraism) containing a remarkable description of the whole ordered series of images that comprised the patient's vision. Jung asked himself; 'How on earth is it possible that this fellow came into possession of that vision?'[27]

Jung observed that many of the motifs and symbols expressed in the dreams and unconscious material of his patients were in fact evident in folklore and mythology, of which such patients had no knowledge. For him only a collective unconscious dimension could explain this remarkable coincidence and, as well, why so many of the same symbols and mythological motifs were to be found in different and unrelated cultures across the world. For him this was evidence that much of what it is to be human is universal, regardless of culture, and has been so throughout human history.[28]

Concerning archetypes and their representations in mythology and religion, Jung argued that the universal occurrence of symbols and motifs in so many separate mythologies 'should be enough to suggest a theory of a common psychic heritage for mankind'.[29] Such symbols and motifs point back to the archetypes or patterns within the collective unconscious, which they make present.

In mythology, a symbol functions as a bridge – the means of linking two worlds or dimensions of reality: the 'infinite and the ultimate with the finite and the concrete'; the 'everyday world of "now" and the world as it was in the beginning, in the "time of perfection"'. 'For all symbols there are these two aspects: there is the concrete, this world, conscious aspect, and there is the *other* to which it points and that it, in some way, also makes present'.[30]

A myth in Jung's terminology is quite the opposite of

something 'false', 'untrue', or 'not real' (which is what the term in everyday usage suggests). Rather, it refers to something infinitely true; it refers to a special kind of story regarded by indigenous cultures as sacred, because it describes:

> *...a greater, usually primordial reality, and certainly a more relevant reality by which the present world was to be evaluated.*[31]

A myth helps describe 'how life is and how life is to be responded to'.[32]

Jung maintained that myths 'provide a sense of wider meaning to one's existence'; they are what raise us above self-centred materialism; they are living truths describing psychic realities.[33] 'A tribe's mythology is its living religion whose loss is always and everywhere, even among the civilized, a moral catastrophe'.[34]

Myths have always supplied models for human behaviour; they point to a wider reality – one that goes beyond limited personal experience. Through them:

> *In all places and in all times, people have found values that gave significance to their lives and lifted them out of the humdrum of daily existence. And the only way this kind of transcendent value can be talked about is in stories – the language of myth and symbols.*[35]

Perhaps the most important thing that can be said of myths and mythic symbols is that they have an extraordinary *participative quality*, the ability to make present another reality through their participation in that reality.[36] Neojungians believe them to be a 'visible', 'living' and accessible link with archetypal potentials, able to point men towards and connect them with the inspiriting, patterning, and transformative sources of the most noble masculinity.

In recent times there has been a resurgence of interest in mythology in the West, championed by people such as Joseph Campbell (author of books like *The Power of Myth* and *The Hero with a Thousand Faces*), and authors involved in the American mythopoetic men's movement, such as Robert Bly, Robert Johnson, James Hillman, Robert Moore, Douglas Gillette, and many others. A rich and varietal panoply of mythologies, mythic characters and images have been popularised as the means of accessing and experiencing masculine archetypes. North American Indian, Arthurian, Greek, Middle Eastern, Scandinavian, Indian, and Christian Celtic mythologies are amongst those that have been co-opted for this endeavour.

Perhaps the most popular and enduring myths in Western Society are those of the Arthurian tradition. They tell of Kind Arthur and Avalon, of Merlin and the Grail, and of Otherworldly women who were its guardians. Within this tradition are the great chivalric epics that tell of brave and noble knights, their adventures through dark and impenetrable forests, facing strange and terrible adversaries. Arthurian scholar, John Matthews, says of the Arthurian myths:

> *...these are not simply stories. Within them lies a depth and variety of human experience which derives from a timeless dimension. Taken as part of the continuing Western mystery tradition, they form a background to daily living in a unique and extraordinary way.*[37]

Matthews believes that meditating upon the images and events of the Arthurian legend can deepen an awareness of their archetypal nature but also, more importantly, can invite the transformative power of the archetypes they present into human experience.[38]

This belief in the efficacy, role, and accessibility of

archetypes is (as already noted) fundamental to much of the recent Neojungian literature concerned with masculinity and male development. Amongst the most popular exponents of this thinking are Robert Moore and Douglas Gillette, authors of the book *King, Warrior, Magician, Lover*. These authors contend that the four archetypes of King, Warrior, Magician, and Lover, are recurrent in different mythologies, and can be taken to represent:

> *...the building blocks... the four fundamental configurations which, in dynamic relationship, constitute the deep structures of the mature male psyche...* [39]

Quite apart from the idea of archetypes (and whether one chooses to accept what is claimed about them), Moore and Gillette's characterisation of these mythic entities – particularly their necessary interdependent and dynamic relationship, as a model of mature manhood, has both merit and relevance within our present discussion, and our overarching theme: Reconstituting the Manhood Ideal.

Before examining Moore and Gillette's archetypal schema, it is important to include a couple of qualifications that need to be borne in mind in relation to the way archetypes and archetypal images should be viewed (qualifications emphasised by exponents of Jung).

Firstly, archetypal images and their characterisations should not be regarded as or mistaken for the archetypes to which they point, or that they (in symbolical form) make present. They should be considered a bridge to the archetypal source but not be confused with it:

> *Mistaking a specific archetypal image for... the ultimate source... leads to idolatry, a decisive and dangerous mistake widespread in the histories of religions and cultures.*[40]

Secondly, how an archetype is experienced in an individual human psyche will always be specific or peculiar to that person and 'will be drawn from his or her total experience, but the archetype itself is something universal'.[41]

Neojungians Propose Archetypes as the Source of the Mature Masculine

Carl Jung proposed that every person's psyche is grounded in and connected with what he termed the *collective unconscious* – the vast repository containing the entire historical and cultural heritage and wisdom of humanity – the source of the instinctual forces of the psyche, and the forms that regulate them, the *archetypes.*

Neojungians believe that the attributes of exemplary manhood are potent and enduring because they originate in masculine archetypes.

Masculine archetypes (or 'potentials') are thought to be a potential patterning, shaping and organising force within the psyche. Their effect has been likened to that of a magnet beneath a sheet of paper, able to rearrange iron filings on top of the sheet along the lines of magnetic force.

Archetypes, though unseen, can be experienced in their effects. We can observe something of their shapes and patterns through their effects or manifestation, in art, poetry, music, religion, in our scientific discoveries, as well as in our patterns of behaviour, thought and feeling.
Neojungians suggest that why we don't see more evidence of masculine archetypes orientating manhood to be mature manhood, is because, in a variety of ways, men are blocked from experiencing them due to such things as: the loss of ritual processes, societal demands on the male role, anti-male attitudes, a scarcity of mature all-male environments, and the overshadowing of myth and mythic imagination by rationalism and materialism.

The symbols and motifs of numerous mythologies and religions point back to the archetypes or patterns within the collective unconscious.

In mythology, symbols function as a bridge and link between two dimensions of reality, the infinite and the ultimate to the finite and the concrete. That to which they point they also in some way make present.

Myths provide a more relevant reality by which to evaluate our present world; they describe how life is and how best we can respond to it; they supply models for human behaviour; they raise us above self-centered materialism; they describe psychic realities.

Myths and mythic symbols are believed to be a 'visible', 'living' and accessible link with archetypal potentials, able to point men towards and connect them with the transformative sources of the most noble masculinity.

Moore and Gillette suggest four fundamental archetypes which constitute the deep structures of the mature masculine psyche: King, Warrior, Magician and Lover. These authors emphasise the essential dynamic relationship between these archetypes, and that they give rise to mature manhood only if they are in proper relation to each other, and manifest in the male psyche in a complementary and dynamic tension.

Archetypal images and characterisations should not be regarded as or mistaken for the archetypes to which they point, or that they (in symbolical form) make present.

The experience of archetypes by an individual will always be specific to that person, and will draw on their total experience, though the archetype is universal.

Table 13

Moore and Gillette detail a range of mature masculine attributes associated with or emanating from what they have observed to be the four recurrent fundamental archetypes of King, Warrior, Magician, and Lover:

King

Considered primal in all men, this archetype may be thought of as first in importance, because it underlies and incorporates the variety of other masculine archetypes in perfect balance. The good and generative King is also a good Warrior, a positive Magician, and a great Lover.[42] Though first in importance, for most men, its attributes are often realised after those of other archetypes. King is central; King is wisdom.

The King archetype 'possesses the qualities of order, of reasonable and rational patterning, of integration and integrity in the masculine psyche'.[44]

'It stabilises chaotic emotion and out-of-control behaviour.

It gives stability and centredness.

It brings calm.

It mediates vitality, life-force, and joy.

It brings maintenance and balance.

It defends our own sense of inner order, our own integrity of being and of purpose, our own central calmness about who we are, and our essential unassailability and certainty in our masculine identity.

It looks upon the world with a firm but kindly eye.

It sees others in their weakness and all their talent and worth; it honours them and promotes them; it guides them and nurtures them toward their own fullness of being.

> It is not envious because it is secure, as the King, in its own worth.
>
> It rewards and encourages creativity in us and in others'.[45]

'In its central incorporation and expression of the Warrior, it represents aggressive might when that is what is needed when order is threatened. It also has the power of inner authority. It knows and discerns (its Magician aspect) and acts out of this deep knowingness. It delights in us and in others (its Lover aspect) and shows this delight through words of authentic praise and concrete actions that enhance our lives'.[46]

Warrior

When the Warrior energy functions in isolation, unrelated to other archetypes, the results can be disastrous.[47] 'Around the planet, warfare in our century has reached such monstrous and pervasive proportions that aggressive energy itself is looked upon with deep suspicion and fear'.[48] But when the Warrior energy is in right relation with the other mature masculine energies, 'something truly splendid emerges'.[49]

When the energies of Warrior and King combine in a man he will be seen to consciously steward the 'realm', and his 'decisive actions, clarity of thinking, discipline, and courage are, in fact, creative and generative'.[50]

Warrior and Magician brought into right relation in a man will enable him to achieve informed, constructive, disciplined mastery and control over himself and his 'weapons' – to properly utilise and direct power in the accomplishment of worthy goals.[51]

Warrior and Lover energies brought into right relation in a man will engender 'compassion and a sense of connectedness with all things'.[52] 'The Lover is the masculine energy that brings a man into relatedness with human beings...The Lover makes the man... compassionate at the same time that he is doing his duty'.[53]

The Warrior in his fullness will exhibit characteristics such as:

Living life nobly and with courage

'A stance towards life that rouses, energises and motivates'.[54]

Taking the offensive (rather than being defensive) in the face of life's tasks and problems.

Knowing, through being awake, alert, clear thinking, focussed in mind and body, and by being discerning of what aggressiveness is appropriate in particular circumstances.[55]

Does not play hero. Knows his limitations and acknowledges his vulnerabilities.

'Is aware of and knows the shortness of life and how fragile it is...This means he engages life. He never withdraws from it'.[56]

Concern with skill, self-development, discipline and

control, 'both inner and outer, psychological and psysical'.[57]

Actions are never overdone, never dramatic for the sake of drama; the Warrior never acts to reassure himself that he is as potent as he hopes he is'.[58]

An 'unconquerable spirit...great courage...is fearless, takes responsibility for his actions'.[59]

A 'transpersonal commitment'. Is loyal to an ideal, a cause, a people, a task, a nation.

'...the psyche of a man...accessing the Warrior is organised around his central commitment'.[60]

'...loyalty...and his sense of duty are to something beyond and other than himself and his own concerns'.[61]

Managing his emotions. Acting not out of emotion or impulsiveness, but in service to his ideal.[62]

Warrior energy is universally present in men. It cannot simply be voted out. It must be encouraged to develop into its fullness and to be integrated and in right relation with the other archetypes of the mature masculine.[63]

Magician

'The energies of the Magician archetype, wherever and whenever we encounter them, are twofold. The Magician is the knower and he is the master of technology. The Magician is an initiate of secret and hidden knowledge of all kinds. All knowledge that takes special training to acquire is the province of the Magician energy'.[64]

The Magician/Shaman of ancient cultures (and of those that still acknowledge this role) was the one who guided ritual and initiatory processes. He was the ritual elder, the one who could see not only into the depths of nature but of human beings. He was a seer and a prophet, a practitioner of the sacred; he understood the links between the unseen world and the world of human beings and nature. He was powerful in his knowledge, and was responsible for the moral use of this power.[65]

Ours is the age of the Magician – 'at least in his materialistic concern with understanding and having power over nature. But in terms of...psychological, or spiritual initiatory process, the Magician energy seems to be in short supply. Ours is an age...of personal and gender identity chaos. And chaos is always the result of inadequate accessing of the Magician in some vital area of life'.[66]

The Magician archetypical energy exhibits characteristics such as:

Awareness, insight, and knowledge of things not immediately apparent.

Trustworthiness in the right use of knowledge and the moral use of its power.

Consciously uses knowledge, technical proficiency and insight for the benefit of self and others.

Clarity of thinking; decision making with careful insightful reflective deliberation.

Introversion: 'the capacity to detach from the inner and outer storms and to connect with deep inner truths and resources'.[67]

Being centered and grounded, 'not easily pushed and pulled around'; '...is immovable in its stability, centeredness, and emotional detachment'.[68]

Can enter ritual or 'sacred' space using means such as music, movement, meditation, and experiencing and 'being one with' nature.[69]

Sees evil for what and where it is when it masquerades as goodness.

The ability to deflate arrogance, to 'bring down to earth', and to help men grow fully into masculine maturity (as was the role of King Arthur's Magician, Merlin).[70]

The ability to work with and provide ritual and initiatory processes.

Helps to link seen and unseen realities.[71]
Is a seer, contemplative, prophet, priest, and mediator of the 'sacred', the 'other-worldly'.[72]

Lover
The Lover is the primal energy of vividness, aliveness, and passion. 'It is the energy of sensitivity to the outside environment'. It expresses 'the function of the psyche that is trained in on all the details of sensory

experience, the function that notices colours and forms, sounds, tactile sensations, and smells'. The Lover also monitors the changing textures of the inner psychological world as it responds to incoming sensory impressions.[73] It is the archetype of healthy embodiment of being in the world of sensuous pleasure and in one's own body without shame.[74] All artistic and creative endeavour draws on Lover energy. This energy is the source of spirituality: 'In the mystical tradition, which underlies and is present within all the world's religions, the Lover energy, through the mystics, intuits the ultimate oneness in daily life, while it still dwells in a mortal finite man'.[75]

The Lover archetype exhibits characteristics such as:

Seeing all things bound to each other in mysterious ways.[76]

Sensitivity to all inner and outer things.[77]

A sense of compassionate and empathic connectedness with all people and the physical world...'sees the world in a grain of sand'...but also 'feels that this is so'.[78]

Aesthetic consciousness...'experiences everything, no matter what it is, aesthetically. All of life is art...and evokes subtly nuanced feelings'.[79]

'Recognising no boundaries'. Wants to live out the connectedness that is felt 'with the world inside, in the context of...powerful feelings, and outside, in the context of...relationships with other people'.[80]

'Feeling joy and delight in all the sensory experiences of life'.[81]

By feeling one with others and with the world, their pain is also felt. 'Other people may be able to avoid pain, but the man in touch with the Lover must endure it. He feels the painfulness of being alive – both for himself and others'.[82]

Unconventionality: resisting socially created boundaries and conventional moralisms; is in a sense opposed to law and advocates passionate experience.[83]

Artistic and creative capacity expressed in all kinds of professions and human endeavours.

The experience of seeing and feeling the world as vividly alive and meaningful – along with its pain and sorrow.[84]

Men appropriately accessing the Lover archetype... feel 'related, connected, alive, enthusiastic, compassionate, empathic, energised, and romantic about life, goals, work and achievements'. 'It is the Lover which gives us a sense of meaning...spirituality'. 'It is the Lover that is the source of our longing for a better world for ourselves and others. He it is who is the idealist and the dreamer'.[85]

'The Lover keeps the other masculine energies human, loving and related to each other and to the real life situation of human beings struggling in a difficult world'. Without the Lover, the other archetypes are '...all essentially detached from life. They need the

Lover to energise them, to humanise them, and to give them their ultimate purpose – love'. But the Lover cannot do without them either. The Lover needs the order, structure and boundaries the King defines; the Lover needs the Warrior energy, in order to be able to act decisively and to detach; it needs the Magician '...to help him back off from the ensnaring effect of his emotions, in order to reflect, to get a more objective perspective on things, to disconnect – enough at least to see the big picture and to experience the reality beneath the seeming'.[86]

References

1. Hillman, J., **The Soul's Code: In Search of Character and Calling** (Australia, Random House, 1996) p. 32

2. Moore, R. and Gillette, D., **King Warrior Magician Lover: Rediscovering The Archetypes of The Mature Masculine** (U.S.A Harper Collins, 1990)

3. Frankl, V., **Man's Search For Meaning: An Introduction to Logotherapy** (London, Hodder and Stoughton, 1976) p. 106

4. Op.cit., Hillman, p. 32

5. Campbell, J., (ed.) **The Portable Jung** (New York, Viking, 1971)

6. Eliade, M., **Patterns In Comparative Religion** (U.S.A. The World Publishing Co., 1963)

7. Wallace, C., **Jung and Christianity: The Challenge of Reconciliation** (Australia, Collins Dove, 1989)

8. Campbell, J., **The Power of Myth** (London, Anchor Books, 1988)

9. Kipnis, A., **Knights Without Armor: A Practical Guide For Men In Quest of Masculine Soul** (U.S.A., Jeremy, P. Tarcher, 1991) p. 98

10. Keen, S., **Fire In The Belly** (U.S.A., Bantam Books, 1991) chapter 11

11. Ibid., p. 156

12. Ibid., p. 457

13. Ibid., p. 162

14. Ibid., pp. 165-167

15. Ibid., pp. 168-170

16 Ibid., pp. 171-172

17. Ibid., pp. 172-175

18. Ibid., p. 170

19. Ibid., p. 180

20. Ibid., p. 183

21. Ibid., p. 184

22. Op. cit., Moore & Gillette, p. 9

23. **The Collected Works of C.G. Jung** Read, Sir Herbert, et al. (eds.) Hull, R.F.C. (trans.) [2d ed. rev., Bollingen Series XX] (Princeton, N.J.: Princeton University Press, 1970) VIII, p. 158

24. Op. cit., Moore & Gillette, pp. 10-11

25. Ibid., p. 44

26. Ibid., Part I, chapters 1-6

27. Op. cit., The Collected Works of C.G. Jung, XVIII, p. 142

28. Op. cit., Wallace, p. 58

29. Ibid.

30. Ibid., p. 54

31. Ibid., p. 59

32. Ibid.

33. Jung, C., **Man and His Symbols** (New York, Dell Publishing Company, 1964) p. 42

34. Op. cit., The collected Works of C.G Jung, IX (I), p. 154

35. Op. cit., Wallace, pp. 64-65

36. Ibid., p. 53

37. Matthews. J., **The Arthurian Tradition** (U.K., Element Books, 1994) p. 7

38. Ibid., p. 84

39. Op. cit., Moore & Gillette, preface, p. xi

40. Grof, S., **The Cosmic Game: Explorations In The Frontiers of Human Consciousness** (U.S.A., Hill of Content, 1998) p. 24

41. Op. cit., Wallace, p. 19

42. Op. cit., Moore & Gillette, p. 49

43. Ibid.

44. Ibid., pp. 61-62

45. Ibid., p. 62

46. Ibid.

47. Ibid., p. 87

48. Ibid., p. 75

49. Ibid., p. 86

50. Ibid.

51. Ibid.

52. Ibid.

53. Ibid.

54. Ibid., pp. 78-79

55. Ibid., pp. 79-80

56. Ibid., pp. 80-82

57. Ibid., p. 83

58. Ibid.

59. Ibid.

60. Ibid., p. 84

61. Ibid., p. 85

62. Ibid.

63. Ibid., pp. 75-79

64. Ibid., p. 98

65. Ibid., pp. 98-99

66. Ibid., p. 102

67. Ibid., p. 108

68. Ibid.

69. Ibid., p. 110

70. Ibid., pp. 100-101

71. Ibid., pp. 98-99

72. Ibid., p. 99

73. Ibid., p. 120

74. Ibid., p. 121

75. Ibid., pp. 130 & 124

76. Ibid., p. 121

77. Ibid., p. 122

78. Ibid.

79. Ibid.

80. Ibid.

81. Ibid., p. 124

82. Ibid., p. 125

83. Ibid., pp. 126 & 127

84. Ibid., p. 130

85. Ibid., p. 140

86. Ibid., pp. 140 & 14

7

Resources for Transformation and Transition

It has been proposed that the appropriate socialisation, psychological and moral development of boys, and the attainment of mature manhood by boys and men, are only possible based on the full repertoire of manly attributes associated with mature manhood; those characterised by mature *man psychology* rather than immature *boy psychology*. Only out of the wholeness of a properly constituted manhood ideal can boys be adequately and appropriately prepared for manhood; only in honest pursuit of this ideal can men lay claim to true manliness. Such an ideal alone provides the threshold and pathway for boys' and men's quest for honourable manhood. What might be considered to be the core attributes of this ideal have been noted and discussed.

The question that remains is: By what means can boys (aspiring to manhood) and men be inspired and enlisted by this ideal, and experience being launched or initiated into a commitment to and pursuit of it – in order for its attributes to be realised in them and lived out in everyday life?

In response to this question, we need to explore a number of further topics, including: the meaning, elements and contemporary utility of initiatory process, the role of mentors, and some possibilities of our own Australian social context.

THE RELEVANCE AND ROLE OF INITIATION

With so much emphasis in our society on child health and welfare, childhood development, child rearing, parenting and education, it seems extraordinary – and bewilderingly contradictory, that when it comes to the profoundly consequential matter of transition from childhood to adulthood, the young are left largely unsupported; they are, in effect, abandoned and left to their own devices. The problem, of course, is that their own devices originate from their own immaturity, and are not informed by the wisdom or attributes of mature adulthood.

It was noted earlier that boys who are left without this assistance frequently resort to means of self-initiation that are dangerous and often harmful to themselves and sometimes to others. Their desperate yet misguided bid to prove themselves worthy of inclusion in the adult world of men is expressed through the abuse of alcohol, through many forms of dangerous risk taking, through violence, aggression, destructiveness, trophy-sex, public posturing, self-aggrandisement, and by using and abusing others. As was also noted, should we be surprised that we have managed to produce such a large number of impulsive, uninitiated pseudo-warriors? Such attempts at self-initiation usually merely result in initiation into a more toughened, strident and aggressive version of boy psychology.

Other examples of ineffectual or pseudo-initiation are those with often more evident ritual elaboration, and an institutional or defined social basis. Street and motor cycle gangs commonly engage members in ritual initiation, but do not produce men; military training may have the potential to produce discipline and character (and often has), but too frequently its initiations have been entrusted to 'adolescents' who are men only in age and who, through gratuitous humiliations and brutality, produce no different effect in those they initiate. Many male sporting clubs – football, rugby, and others, also incorporate some rituals of progression and reward that constitute something of an initiatory process. They too have much potential to produce self-discipline and good character, but again have not infrequently given rise to social cultures that are anything but mature. Often they have been associated with drunken brawling, disrespect for women, and an aggressive and impulsive pack mentality. Mature men do not behave in these ways; they have no need or liking for hostile, threatening, disrespectful, controlling or gratuitously violent or aggressive behaviours. Such behaviours are a pretense of manhood and manifest evidence of uninitiated boy psychology.

The problem of unsupported and consequently unsuccessful transition from boy psychology to man psychology is obviously not just one experienced at the time of manhood-aspiring adolescence; it is carried into and throughout male adult life. Certainly, processes of natural maturation through successive experiences of trial and error, and reinforcement and reward associated with pressure to assume and perform adult responsibilities, shape and temper personality and behaviour. But to what extent do they effect a fundamental shift from boy to man? The fact that this doesn't happen for many men in a satisfactory way might suggest that some kind of transformative initiatory process is of critical importance, not only for adolescent boys aspiring to manhood, but as well for men that have never quite succeeded in making this essential transition:

> *Lacking adequate models of mature men and lacking the societal cohesion and institutional structures for actualising ritual process, it's "every*

> *man for himself". And most of us fall by the wayside, with no idea what it was that was the goal of our gender-drive or what went wrong in our strivings. We just know we are anxious, on the verge of feeling impotent, helpless, frustrated, put down, unloved and unappreciated, often ashamed of being masculine. We cave into a dog-eat-dog world, trying to keep our work and relationships afloat, losing energy, or missing the mark.[1]*

Many men remain boys, failing to progress to mature manhood, not because they want to, but because no one has shown them how. Sadly, no small number of men have succumbed to the persuasive pressure of feminisation and demasculinisation as a promised (yet illusory) path to a better kind of maleness. But as Moore and Gillette rightly point out:

> *We do not need, as some feminists are saying, less masculine power. We need more. But we need more of the mature masculine; we need more man psychology.[2]*

Ours is a culture that is confused about gender and has failed to clarify a profile of mature masculinity. It has largely dispensed with the services of myth and ritual, and has shown a tendency to discard the wisdom of the past in favour of the 'more intelligent new'. But it would seem that we have, in matters of human maturity and character, become clever without wisdom. We have allowed the traits of boy psychology and girl psychology (albeit clothed with modern sophistication) to gain ascendancy and masquerade as adulthood.

Though we would be hard-pressed to find men in our culture that have experienced an effective *formal* ritual initiation into the manhood ideal or man psychology (except perhaps in non-western and indigenous groups), there are of course men who have experienced initiatory transformation; men who have genuinely struggled to attain to an honourable manhood, with little or no assistance, except for their own search for and utilisation of available means.

Why haven't such men been more noticeable? Probably for at least two reasons: firstly, we simply don't have a term in common parlance by which to identify and validate them; secondly, it has been considered politically incorrect to do so for fear of reinforcing 'traditional masculinity'. Such men have thus become part of what might be termed a *masculine diaspora* – scattered abroad and self-protectively 'invisible' in a prevailing culture which has discouraged the 'citizenship' of masculine, and has sought actively to dismantle and be rid of masculine culture.

Such means that men have found and utilized to help them effect a transition from boyhood to more mature manhood are akin to some of the basic elements to be found in the more complex and integrated 'tapestries' of traditional initiatory rituals.[3] Identifying these elements can provide us with a potential resource to assist us in our contemporary need of transformative initiatory experience – in the absence of a widely recognised, socially authorised and validated ritual initiatory process.

KEY ELEMENTS OF TRADITIONAL INITIATION

In tribal societies there are highly specific notions about adulthood, and carefully constructed rituals for enabling boys, when the time is right, to make the transition into manhood.[4] As one of the most ancient of rites, initiation marks the crossing of a threshold into a new consciousness, a new knowledge, responsibility, and life orientation. The major themes of initiation are suffering/testing, 'death', and rebirth. But it must also achieve the revelation of the sacred; the candidate must pass beyond the natural mode (that of the uninitiated child) and gain access to and awareness of the cultural mode – the tribe's mythological and cultural traditions; he must be introduced to spiritual values.[5]

Boys must be 'twice born' to learn how to function 'soulfully' and rationally in the adult world, leaving childhood behind.[6] Man psychology cannot come into being without a symbolic, psychological 'death'. 'Old ways of being and doing and thinking and feeling must ritually "die", before the new man can emerge'.[7] The achievement of initiation, if it is effective, is that a man becomes what he is, and he is launched into what he should become.[8] It is interesting how this is mirrored in Christianity (which borrowed the vocabulary of initiation from earlier mystery religions), in its sacrament of baptism, which is symbolic of death and rebirth (or resurrection) to a new life, initiation into the Christian mysteries, and into both an awareness of, and commitment to, living according to spiritual values. Also, as with initiation in tribal societies, baptism is generally followed by ongoing instruction in the values and principles that should govern behaviour, and must at all times be honoured.[9/10]

Very importantly, the initiation process recognises the enormous energies that are released in young men at the onset of puberty. It has been recognised by tribal elders since time began, that the vitality and volatility of young males can bring new life or death to a society. If their energies are not correctly orientated and directed, if they are not linked with and trained to be expressed through attributes derivative of man psychology, they will likely be an antisocial force within the community, or will manifest destructively later on in the roles of husband and father.[11]

In Western society, it would appear that we are unconcerned with the damage that young men may do to themselves and others, for want of careful adult guidance, initiatory orientation, and mentoring. What are loosely termed 'rites of passage', in our society, have little influence in achieving a fundamental shift in consciousness. They are largely only markers of advancing age, signs of an ill-defined expectation of adulthood. But who spells out what is expected of a man, when such markers are not accompanied by or linked to the guiding values, principles and attributes of mature manhood?

It is significant that ceremony and celebration accompany school graduations, a 21st birthday, or graduation from university, but in what ways are age and the successful acquisition of knowledge clearly associated with moral responsibility, or imbued with moral consciousness? What kind of initiatory process provides a sound basis of responsibility for permitting young men at a certain age to drive a motor vehicle, drink alcohol, engage in sexual relationships, perhaps marry, or father children? And yet any of these freedoms if exercised with immaturity can be disastrous.

Far from being archaic or anachronistic, initiation appears to be vitally important to nurturing positive, generative and responsible male citizenship. Not only so, but it invests in and encourages an internal behavioural locus of control, rather than society having to depend so heavily on the 'blunt object' of the deterrent and punitive functions of law, to try to contain and control the irrepressible energies of youth – and of the not so youthful who have never grown up.

Ritual initiatory process still survives in tribal cultures of Africa, South America, the islands of the South Pacific and many other places, including amongst some Aborigines in Australia.[12] Broadly speaking, the Australian Aboriginal initiation process (observable across many different Aboriginal tribal groups), has four main phases (which are similarly reflected in other initiatory traditions around the world). First, under the guidance of a tribal elder, the preparation of a sacred ritual place or 'sacred ground' must occur. This place is sealed from the influence of the outside world, and especially from the influence of women. This is where the men (and the boys to be initiated) must remain in isolation until the ritual is completed. Only once the novices are considered to have satisfactorily completed their testing, and have been reborn (by men) as men, are they released from the sacred place. Second, the novices are separated from their mothers and, in general, from all women. There is no longer scope or opportunity for puerile regression, or seeking protection or refuge amongst women. Third, the novices are segregated in the bush or in a special isolated camp, where they are instructed in the religious and mythological traditions of the tribe. They are shown enactments of episodes of the great tribal myths. Fourth, the novices are put through an ordeal, usually circumcision, subincision, having a tooth pulled out, or perhaps wounding of the upper body (consequenting subsequent scarring), or pulling out of hair. For the duration of the initiation the novices must behave strictly according to tradition and instruction.[13/14/15] Instruction in the ways of the tribe's law and spirituality continue beyond the completion of initiation.[16]

East African tribal societies incorporate much the same elements in their initiation rites as we have observed of the Australian Aborigines. A conspicuous difference though is in the drawn-out transitional testing adolescents, or *moran,* must experience. The Samburu and Masai tribes are well documented examples of societies that demand a long period of initiatory testing, training and preparation for manhood. Commencing at around the age of fourteen or fifteen, adolescents commence the period of moranhood by experiencing a traumatic circumcision procedure. They are taken off, away from the village, to a preselected place where they see out the time of their long initiation, going through a series of rituals and tests, perfecting their skills, and learning the ways of their culture.[17]

The Masai place a strong emphasis on physical courage – being able and prepared to confront dangerous animals, and protect the tribe against marauding enemies. In both the Samburu and Masai, initiation also aims to produce a new consciousness of economic independence and responsibility. A high point in a boy's moranhood is the sacrifice of his first Ox and the distribution of its meat. This marks him as a 'worthy man', one who is no longer just a consumer, but a provider of meat – indicating responsible adult manhood. As with the Australian Aborigines, these societies consider a young man only ready for marriage once having been initiated.[18]

The theme of generativity (being no longer just a consumer but a provider of things), represents an important theme in the initiation rite (or *bartaman*) of Hindu Nepalese society. The incorporation of a young man into caste society requires that henceforth he becomes responsible for his own actions, but as well moves from material dependence on others to economic responsibility. It is interesting to note that, in Western society, this aspect of childhood is becoming increasingly protracted. Young people are staying at home and, in effect, are remaining dependants for much longer than they used to.[19] Certainly our affluence permits this, but it is also indicative of how distinctions between childhood and adulthood have become diluted and unclear.

Common within mythologies is the idea of quest, or *vision quest*, a term especially popularised through recent Western interest in Native American Traditions. Vision quest is an expression of the archetypal heroic journey, enacted in religious pilgrimages, mythological tales (such as that of the search for the Holy Grail), and in contemporary Vision Quest programs, often conducted in a wilderness area.[20/21/22]

Because these programs often serve as a modern rite of initiation into deeper levels of adulthood (rather than a social or religious group), their nature, and that of the mythological idea of *quest*, is worthy of comment.

In mythology, the quest is about going in search of something of great value and use – a vision, insight, or resource. The journey characteristically requires leaving the world one is in (with its familiarity and security), and venturing, 'into a depth or into a distance or up to a height', in search of what is missing in one's consciousness and awareness, in the world formerly inhabited. On attaining the goal of this quest (securing the sought after vision, insight or resource), the challenge becomes holding on to it, on returning back to one's social world.[23]

Modern Vision Quest programs are commonly a synthesis of elements of ancient quest traditions and the self-development tools of transpersonal psychology. They are conducted to enable individuals to put their lives on a path that allows for both self-fulfilment and genuine service to others – a deeper level of authentic adulthood; they encourage people to connect with their 'deepest selves', beyond (and leaving behind) current old ways of defining themselves, in order to attain to greater authenticity and to discover new passion and a more human and meaningful approach to life. Through their emphasis on solitude and encountering nature, they attempt to provide conditions conducive to *unitive experience*, whereby individuals may experience deeply their oneness with and dependence on the natural world, flowing on to a deep sense of interdependence and connectedness with all other people and creatures, thus providing an experiential basis of moral consciousness.[24]

The components of these programs (and there are many variations) may include a preparatory time at a retreat centre, followed by a time alone in nature (often several days and nights) with solitude and fasting – in order to achieve the displacement of everyday consciousness. The use of ceremonial processes and self-awareness/insight skills (taught at the time of preparation) are also common components. The Vision Quest is then concluded with reincorporation and consolidation activities, to enable the person to 'embody' what they have gained and return to everyday life.[25]

The enduring challenge of the Vision Quest is that, in order to found or create something new, one has to leave the old, the known, and go in quest of the seed potential that is capable of germination – capable of growing into something new and better.

Whatever may be said of the potential efficacy of initiatory process, it is not a guarantee of masculine maturity. When effective, it produces a sufficient transformation of consciousness for the adoption of and allegiance to the attributes of a manhood ideal. Its efficacy will always need to be judged by its outcomes, evident in character and conduct. Nor is initiation (of the kind we have noted) the only means by which boys and men can experience a transformation of consciousness resulting in a marked positive change in self-insight, awareness, attitude and behaviour; there are a variety of spiritual and psychological practices that may achieve this effect (such as meditation, contemplation, and methods of depth and transpersonal psychology). Nor should we be sceptical about the possibility that some individuals will simply experience spontaneous life-changing 'awakenings'. Nevertheless, the design of initiation (which includes certain methods in common with non-initiatory spiritual and psychological practices) is specific to the task of achieving transition from boy psychology to man psychology – from boyhood to manhood. It has, across time and different cultures, been the preferred and pre-eminent means for achieving this transition.

Initiation assumes and necessitates a *community* of men, in which there are those ('elders') who can expound the attributes of the manhood ideal, and who exemplify and live out (albeit imperfectly) a vision of mature manhood. It is the community of men that alone can set the stage for, support, guide, and validate the initiatory process; it is this community that is needed to make the benefits of initiation sustainable, through ongoing reinforcement, instruction, example and encouragement. To be initiated is to cross the threshold not only into manhood but also into acceptance and membership in the community of men.

In tribal societies, rites of initiation are instruments in their endeavour to sustain themselves. They are not merely aimed at individual transformation, but serve, with the support of the whole society, to continually refresh a society's mythic vision and integrity, enlivening and restating its commitment to its most deeply held values and beliefs. The full efficacy of initiation is only possible with the broadest social validation – including the validation of its ritual apparatus and outcomes.

Elements of Traditional Initiation

<u>Readiness</u>
Usually decided by tribal elders; most commonly initiation is commenced at puberty.

<u>Designated Ritual Place</u>
A sacred 'ritual space' or place is prepared, sealed from the influence of the outside world. Novices are separated from their mothers and all women, and are isolated in this place.

Ordeal and Testing
Commonly involving circumcision or other physical ordeals such as wounding, subincision, having a tooth pulled or knocked out, or being beaten with sticks; tests of endurance, such as facing pain and fear bravely; showing courage in experiencing inescapable solitude, self-confrontation, self-dependence and self-responsibility. Risk and danger are generally measured, monitored and managed by the elders.

Instruction in Values and Beliefs
Under the guidance of elders (or conducted by them), instruction is given in the values, laws, traditions, beliefs – the mythology and spirituality of the tribe. This may occur through mythic re-enactments, ceremony, story-telling and direct instruction.

Reincorporation/Return
Once the initiatory process has been successfully completed, those initiated are brought out of isolation to rejoin the tribe, with the new status and responsibilities of adult men.

Initiation Aims to Produce:

- A 'putting to death' of former ways of being, thinking, feeling, and behaving, in order to permit and facilitate 'rebirth' – the emergence of a man.

- The crossing of a threshold into a new consciousness, awareness, knowledge, and life orientation.

- A new consciousness and acceptance of responsibility for self end others (which may include economic responsibility and independence).

- The revelation of the sacred: passing beyond a natural (uninitiated) awareness, to an awareness of (and access to) the 'cultural mode' – the mythological and spiritual – the ancestral heritage of meaning and values.

- The ability to function 'soulfully' and rationally.

- An understanding of the values, laws, traditions and beliefs of the tribe.

- An adult capacity to face fear, danger and enemies.

- A readiness for the adult responsibility of marriage.

- A transition from boy psychology to man psychology (according to the tribe's culture).

- Initiation into the community of men, and the role of an adult man within the tribe.

- Initiation may be a process that is accomplished over a period of days, weeks, or years.

- Compliance with strict tradition and instruction is demanded throughout the initiatory process.

- Initiation is generally followed by ongoing instruction and learning, and some participation in the process of initiating others.

Table 14

Elements of Modern Vision Quest

Readiness

Participants need themselves to feel ready and open to the experience of Vision Quest. Used as an initiation rite it may include not only adults but is open to older adolescents as well.

Designated Ritual Place

The use of nature and wilderness is a feature of Vision Quest. A retreat centre often provides the first place away from ordinary life, followed by a more remote base camp, from which participants venture away into a place of solitude.

Preparation

The preparation time (which may be several days) is usually spent at the retreat centre and base camp. This is a time spent in self-exploration, and learning to work with the contents of the psyche (such as with dreams, and previously ignored issues and emotions). It is a time for learning to work with the experience of solitude, and in which other ceremonies and practices are used to help participants become centered and open in readiness for the heart of the Quest-time spent seeking alone.

Solitude

This time (usually two or three days) is generally spent alone in nature; it includes fasting, and a concerted quest for desired insight, deepening of awareness, and transformation of consciousness.

<u>Reincorporation/Consolidation</u>
Usually occurs back at the retreat centre or base camp, and involves participants being assisted in consolidating their experience of new insight, awareness and consciousness, in order to return with it back to everyday life.

Vision Quest May Aim To Achieve:

- A fuller initiation into or experience of authentic adulthood.

- Leaving the 'world' one is used to, to go in search of what was missing in one's consciousness in the 'world' formerly inhabited.

- Suspending old ways of defining oneself, to connect with one's deeper 'self', in order to discover new passion, authenticity, and a more meaningful approach to life.

- The displacement of everyday consciousness in order to achieve an openness to unitive experience as a basis for a new moral consciousness.

- Putting life on a path that allows for self-fulfilment and genuine service to others.

- Leaving the known, the old, to go in search of the seed potential capable of growing something new and better.

Table 15

CONTEMPORARY POSSIBILITIES, STRATEGIES AND METHODS

How can initiation be made relevant in our modern, largely demythologised society – a society that appears to have abandoned meaningful ritual process? Moore and Gillette have argued that it is pointless to bemoan our less than ideal parentage and past, or the shortcomings of modern society. They suggest that:

> *What used to be done for us by institutional structures and through ritual process, we now have to do inside ourselves, for ourselves.*[26]

Certainly, we cannot simply mimic or attempt to replicate the ritual formulae and practices specific to other tribal societies – whether ancient or current. And there is arguably little to gain from the 'cultural decadence' of ignoring our own cultural origins and resources (as distant or as meagre as they perhaps appear) in order to pursue another culture's experience, by adopting the trappings of its ritual tradition. We can, however (as already suggested), identify and utilise some of the principles and basic elements common to the way initiation has been and still is practised in many cultures, as a potential resource to assist us in generating the means of transformative initiatory experience for boys and men in our modern society.

We may have neglected the historic myths of the cultures that comprise our modern Western society, but they are not lost – they can never be lost entirely, except perhaps from our conscious view. They and the attributes they represent to us – such as the attributes suggested for a reconstituted manhood ideal, can still inspire boys and men and resonate within them powerfully. They are timeless and enduring, no matter what our modernity or neglect of them. They can be rediscovered and utilised afresh, with immediate contemporary relevance.

There is also much scope for us to go beyond the individual to the collective; for men to set about creating social environments in which individual efforts for transformation and change can be shared, encouraged and enhanced; all-male gatherings and activities – male community, within which the manhood ideal and its attributes can be inculcated, exemplified and declared normative.

With these environments, a reconstituted manhood ideal, some 'raw materials' of initiatory ritual process, and some mythic resources and imagination, it is possible to generate basic ritual initiatory activities that have contemporary relevance.

What is especially needed for boys nearing the age of and aspiring to manhood, is a ritual initiatory process (formulated and conducted by mature men), that can facilitate their transition to manhood (ideally preceded and followed by male mentoring), and clearly mark and celebrate their inclusion and acceptance into the community of men.

To reinforce the privilege and responsibility of their status within the community of men, these young men can then be involved in assisting the older men in the process of initiating others.

As already noted, the attributes of a reconstituted manhood ideal depend for their realisation on a conducive sociocultural environment, which endorses, values, amplifies, reinforces and celebrates them (as is largely necessary for all masculine potentials). The full efficacy of initiation is only possible with broad social support and validation. That we must largely depend on environments created by men, and the *society* of men to try to provide these conditions – until wider societal support can be achieved, does pose limitations. Moreover, what is permissible to include in initiatory process is governed by contemporary standards of safety, duty of care, and risk management that must be observed (in relation to minors and adults).

To whatever extent these limitations can be overcome, it will depend on men seeking the support and achieving the confidence of women in the community; it will depend on men being creative, innovative, experimental and persevering; it will require that men are calmly clear about and sure of their endeavour, and are not na ve about the forceful ideological opposition they may encounter.

One further role that men of a male community can undertake is to develop instruction and basic ritual accompaniments (based on the attributes of the manhood ideal), for the various markers of adult age, freedoms, and responsibilities – in order to give them more meaningful utility as rites of passage, and to imbue them with some moral consciousness (markers such as reaching voting and drinking age, and the traditional 21st birthday).

There is much scope for men to create and reclaim environments, events and opportunities, for reinforcing as normative the attributes of a reconstituted manhood ideal.

Whatever use is made of the idea or elements of initiation, it will need to be congruent and integrated with the attributes of a contemporary manhood ideal; it will need to reflect and be consistent with the needs of our times and our culture; it should emphasise the things we most need to reinforce, encourage and honour. In our use of elements of initiatory process, in our efforts of individual transformation, or in our ritual formulations for use with adolescents (or men), we can reasonably assume that their efficacy (and the overall effect of our initiatory endeavour) will be enhanced, the more of them that can be brought into a complementary and dynamic relation with each other – similar to how learning is enhanced, depending on how many of our faculties can be engaged in the learning process.

The following initiatory elements are proposed for consideration as some contemporary means for transformation and transition – for the necessary shift in consciousness and orientation from boy psychology to man psychology.

Readiness and Decision

Older mature men may need to help decide about the readiness of boys aspiring to manhood before they are engaged in any formal initiatory process. But, whether in boys or men, readiness for change and transition can be fostered and encouraged through the community of men and in men's gatherings. These are not a setting for bleating about victimhood, absent or less than perfect fathers, but where progressive, creative, self-responsible, non-feminising manhood can be nurtured. Here can be presented the powerful influence of example: not some sterile artificial perfection, or condescending pseudo-wisdom, but the example of men who are striving to be better men, through being strong in humility, thoughtful honesty, openness, and the aggressive pursuit of honourable manhood. Here can be demonstrated to young men, personal skills for dealing with everyday issues, problems, and feelings, and social skills for interacting and relating to others appropriately. Here can be grounded the mutually beneficial and challenging relationship of mentors and boys-becoming-men, in which both are progressed in the depth of their manhood.

Men's gatherings hold the promise of providing an environment in which biographies, myths and stories, with messages of character, courage, and humanity, can be expounded; and a culture that inspires noble aspirations and accomplishment – one in which the 'will to meaning', and the will to be an honourable and 'real man', are germinated. Here boys and men need to encounter messages, images and feelings that suggest possibilities. Here they need to find the strength, support, encouragement and safety, to more fully discover their humanity – like in the timeless mythic message in *Star Wars*, when Ben Kenobi instructs Skywalker, in the climax of the last fight, 'Turn off your computer, turn off your machine and do it yourself, follow...trust your feelings'. Such 'letting go' is essential to the readiness that invites the transformation of becoming 'a person of heart and humanity'.[27]

Readiness for change and transition can also arise out of spiritual experience, or out of a sobering, confronting, inspiring, or traumatic life event. It can arise out of extraordinary circumstances into which we find ourselves 'thrown', and in which we perhaps experience a change in perspective, or an altered state of consciousness. But readiness is nothing without decision and action. Promptings, inspiration and opportunities usually pass, or are of little effect, unless we decide to act on them. For example, becoming aware of our 'stuckness' in certain immature patterns of thinking, feeling, or behaviour, will be of little benefit to us unless we decide to pursue the means of change and transformation. As Ralph Waldo Emerson said:

Not in his goals but in his transitions man is great.[28]

One of the most powerful triggers for change in masculine consciousness can be when a man makes a decision to become *a father to himself.*

There is an emphasis in our culture, of late described by James Hillman as the *Parental Fallacy*, which he argues is deadly to individual self-awareness and development, because it suggests that each of us is the result of parenting, and that the primary instrument of our fate is the behaviour of our mother and father, suggesting that:

> *As their chromosomes are ours, so are their mess-ups and attitudes. Their joint unconscious psyche – the rages they suppress, the longings they cannot fulfil, the images they dream at night – basically form our souls, and we can never, ever work through and be free of this determinism.*[29] *I am then a mere effect myself, a result of their causes.*[30]

Hillman also warns that the more we 'cling to the overriding importance of parents' (going beyond what parents can or should be and provide), the less able we are to recognise and benefit from the 'fathering and mothering afforded by the world every day in what it sends our way'.[31]

Symptomatic of men stuck in boy psychology is never quite getting beyond the idea that who they are and what they can become is somehow determined by parentage and parents; or that who they may become must in some way be decided by a parent, or is dependent on them. These are often the men who experience the inertia of unrealised manhood because of their preoccupation with lamenting an absent (in fact or in effect) or less than ideal father; men who have perhaps succumbed to the deadening mediocrity and inauthenticity of too much living in their father's shadow; men who go through life, either unwittingly making choices and ignoring their own aspirations and inclinations in order to win the approval and acceptance of a father, or in rebellion against a father on whom they are resentfully dependent – from whom they have never successfully broken free. In the latter case, such tendencies may be expressed towards a father, but are most commonly played out in relation to other people or institutions that have 'father' characteristics.

For a boy or man to attain to his own sense of manhood, he must not only be 'snatched away from mother's apron strings', but must decisively cease his dependence on or acquiescence to father.

Men (especially young men) will likely need to *best* their father in some way – in order to become respectful and respected equals with them in the world of men. When as men we decide to become a father to ourselves, we move beyond merely asking, 'what would my father do' in this or that situation, to where we ask, 'what would *a* father do? – what as a "father" should *I* do'?

This is no way disparages good parenting; we can scarcely emphasise enough the value of good, caring and responsible parents. But what fathers must abstain from for the sake of their sons, and what sons must not succumb to for their own sake (and the sake of their fathers), is *parentalism* – parenting of a kind that kills individual awareness and development towards manhood. It is for a father to launch his son out of puerility; out of school and home and dependence on parents, into accepting responsibility for his own feelings, choices and behaviours, for setting his own boundaries, and for making his own way in the world as a generative, contributive, and moral adult man.

Deciding to become a father to ourselves should not be understood as opting for independent individualism, or in any way negating our need of the society of others. Rather, it affirms our need to be ourselves and responsible for ourselves, interdependent with but not dependent on others.

Ritual Place/'Sacred Space'
Carefully and thoughtfully designating a place of special significance for the purpose of personal or initiatory transformation both provides the setting and, potentially, can engender the needful sense of expectation for the

change in consciousness that ritual, ceremony, solitude, fasting, meditation and other means may be used to achieve.

Such a 'place apart', whether a room, retreat house, hut, or secluded mountain, desert, woodland, or coastal setting, is vital for clearing a man's head of all the 'clutter', all the demands and 'noise' vying for attention, leaving little room for new awareness or insight, and little time or opportunity to be reflective or introspective.

Such a ritual place would be an essential element in the ritual process of taking a boy (aspiring to manhood) away from the influence, attachments, comforts and 'security' of mother, other women, home and community, to be instructed, tested, and stripped of his boyhood dependence, in order to assimilate the adult responsibilities and consciousness of a man. In tribal societies, such a place (whether a hut or a wilderness), was that into which would-be initiates were driven in order to 'die' to boyhood to be reborn (by men) as men; where the boyish and mundane would give way to, and be displaced by, the archetypal, the spiritual, the revered cultural heritage of the tribe.

There is a sense in which the gathering of men (if for a purpose that engages mature masculinity) may itself create and constitute a ritual place and 'sacred space'. Ironically, it is probably because men-only gatherings have been discouraged (and even strongly opposed by some gender feminists) in recent decades, consequenting their rarity, that they often exhibit conspicuous dynamism – by virtue of how much repressed masculine energy emerges, and how healing and nurturing such gatherings can be for men who have for so long been isolated, and lacking such an environment, in which they can risk being authentically themselves.

More fundamentally though, such gatherings may constitute a 'sacred space' because of their unique capacity to summon, mediate and amplify the most noble and compelling attributes and patterning energies of the masculine psyche. No other setting can so 'inspirit' men with the desire for the kind of manliness for which men have always sacrificed other needs, pleasures, priorities, and even their lives.

It is interesting to note that the link between virtue and manliness that can so powerfully resonate within men is even enshrined in our language. The word virtue is derived from *vir* or man in the Latin. The Latin *virtus* means manliness – manly strength and virtue.[32]

Perhaps most universally indicated as a place suited to ritual work, and as a 'sacred space' most conducive to fruitful solitude, turning inward, and achieving openness in quest of insight, wisdom, and personal transformation, is nature. This setting (and the places of seclusion and retreat men have found in it, or have placed in its 'embrace' – like huts, hermitages, tents and cells), has for all of history been favoured for this work. The Desert Fathers of Egypt, the Celtic nature mystics of Britain, the Franciscan Friars of Italy, the Sufis of Persia, the wandering Poustiniks of Russia, the Orthodox contemplatives of Greece, and Shamans, seekers and mystics of every continent, have found nature invaluable to their earnest quest.

Nature and wilderness have a numinous quality; they have always been known to produce an effect in the human psyche; they have always been able to confer on those who show themselves receptive, a transformative experience. As William Shakespeare declared (in *Troilus and Cressida*):

> *One touch of nature makes the whole world kin.*

What nature has been known to produce in people is not only awe, wonder, and a sense of peace and belonging, but the unitive and transcendental experience of feeling deeply one with nature and all living things – an experience which has also often produced a whole new or significantly expanded sense of moral consciousness and resolve.

Solitude, stillness and silence, together provide another 'sacred space', commonly sought in a setting of nature, but available in any place that is secure against disturbance and interruption, like a room that can be designated 'private'.

Being alone, still and quiet (sometimes combined with fasting – such as in Vision Quest), can be a very effective way of displacing everyday consciousness, in order to become 'empty', open and receptive to new insight, awareness, experience, and the possibility of crossing the threshold into a new consciousness, knowledge, and life orientation. But this can be quite confronting and uncomfortable for those only accustomed to 'noise' and phreneticism. Hence the tendency within spiritual traditions to recommend support and guidance (by those experienced) for those without experience who choose to use these means.

For some people, even the use of a calming relaxation technique can initially be somewhat threatening and anxiety-producing. Silence too, except when it isn't felt during sleep, may be uncomfortable to some. And yet, for those who have become accustomed to it, and who have employed it, it has shown itself to have 'transforming power', and a 'genius of giving everything back to itself'.[33]
In fact, all these elements – solitude, stillness and silence, have a certain genius, permitting the stilling of mind and body, and allowing one, as it were, to become 'empty'. Such emptying and emptiness the mystics of many traditions

believe to be a key to enlightenment and personal transformation, because it is a precondition and invitation for infusion with spirit, the sacred, the Divine, or God – and therefore God-like awareness and moral consciousness. Meister Eckhart (a Christian mystic of the thirteenth century) declared:

> *Preparation is your task and influencing or infusing is His task... you should know that God must be effective and infuse Himself as soon as He finds you ready. Wherever and whenever God finds you ready, He must act and infuse Himself into you.*[34]

In the Western tradition of spirituality, solitude, stillness, and silence were employed both for this purpose of inviting 'God infusion', and as a 'sacred space' in which to most effectively meditate, focus on, and assimilate certain truths and virtues.[35]

Many easily readable books are available in general (but especially religious) book stores on topics such as meditation, contemplation, mysticism, and spiritual practices of a range of spiritual traditions.

Ordeal and Testing

Boys aspiring to manhood, and men struggling with masculine self-identity, have need of deeply felt experiential and social confirmations of initiatory achievement. Such events are generally requisite to engender and cement a mature manly consciousness and orientation. Though we may not wish to advocate ritual initiatory cutting, circumcision, beatings, removal of teeth, drinking of blood, or the requirement to pursue and kill a wild animal, undergoing potent and potentially consciousness changing ordeals and tests is arguably relevant and practicable in our modern setting. If we don't purposefully provide for this, then boys (and men with masculine identity issues), will more often engage in pseudo-initiations that involve needlessly dangerous and foolish posturing, with potential to harm themselves and others.

One might wonder whether the emphases of political correctness and feminisation in many of our schools (where the larger part of boyhood and adolescence are spent), which have misunderstood and prohibited boys' risk-taking (instead of appropriately utilising it), haven't in fact made it more dangerous and intense in its expression, in both competitive and self-initiatory behaviour, in the unmanaged shadows of out-of-school anarchic adolescence. Schools would do well to source their understanding of gender psychology from an informed rather than merely ideological perspective, and to revise their behaviour management rationales and practices, taking account of the particular needs of boys, who are *hyperkinetic* 'square pegs', that on average do not fit in *hypokinetic* 'round holes'!

Fortunately, for boys and men, there are tests and ordeals enough in forms of purposeful risk-taking that can demand great courage, aggressive energy, psychological or physical strength, perseverance, stamina, masculine prowess and virility – without need of physical injury. This is not to suggest a soft option; that would be of no benefit. In fact, the fundamental flaw (and counterproductivity) of adolescent attempts at self-initiation is not that they are too severe (despite often being dangerous), but that they are not severe enough – they are too easy. That they are conspicuously dangerous or daring doesn't make them challenging, difficult or consciousness changing. A boy needs little more than hormones, alcohol, a car, or a reckless and frenzied adolescent group dynamic, to take foolish risks – endangering himself and others. Yet it calls on and brings out a man, when ordeal and testing require risk-taking and endurance that are genuinely self-confronting and purposeful – risk-taking and endurance that demand grappling with 'fierce and painful forces' of decision making and responsibility, change and transition, loss and grief, standing up for what is right – while maintaining fidelity and integrity, and not giving up.

For authentic initiatory experience of ordeal and testing, boys and men perhaps need look no further than their own fears, as an ample source and opportunity: naming, exploring, and acting against fears. This demands courageous risk-taking and endurance, serving not only to assist in the transformation of consciousness, but in the honing of valuable skills for ongoing personal development. As well, it can help pattern and model the right use of masculine power (which should never be frivolously squandered on egoism or illusory self-aggrandisement); it can channel masculine aggression in beneficial ways, such as by forcing back barriers and boundaries of fear, daring to challenge one's assumptions and ideas, bravely permitting the need for humility, compromise or forgiveness, breaking the bonds of one's conformity and inauthenticity, or defying moral indolence and acquiescence, by choosing to do what is right.

Perhaps one of the most perennial fears with which we must contend, which so commonly drives us to 'settle in and make do', when in fact we need to take courage and embrace something new, is transition itself: 'the difficult process of letting go of an old situation, suffering the confusing "nowhere of in-betweenness", and launching forth again in a new situation'.[36] Too often the fear of change, emotional upheaval, pain and grief, can keep us from saying 'yes' to life – yes to a significant opportunity. The great test and ordeal (needful for us to prove ourselves in), essential to our progress, and holding much potential for launching us into a new sense of 'standing on solid ground' within ourselves, and feeling more fully a man, may be: having to bring an end to a toxic and failing relationship (instead of allowing it to generate powerlessness and rage);

getting out of a soul-destroying job, accepting an opportunity for love or for meaning rather than money; or perhaps making a stand on something – a matter of right and principle, regardless of the rejection, ostracism, or change of life's direction it may bring.

Becoming a man and feeling a deep sense of being a man is inseparably linked to experiencing a sense of personal agency, the dignity of causality – making moral and appropriate acts of power. The smallest noble and virtuous act of power can trigger a cascade of inner psychic change. Often, a simple first step can summon the inner resources equal to the task. Or, as Horace put it:

> *He has half the deed done, who has made a beginning.*[37]

Whether in a ritual or ordinary process (which might involve the use of a journal, goal setting, review, and the celebration of achievement), there is much benefit for boys and men in acknowledging, naming, working with, and deciding to overcome fears. But for adolescent boys this is of particular importance, because they generally have much aggressive energy to expend, they have a profound need to establish a viable sense of adult and masculine self-identity, and have many fears and anxieties to face and conquer.

The role of mature men and male mentors may be critical here for guiding boys in informed, purposeful and beneficial risk-taking: enduring the ordeals and succeeding in the tests that can enable mature manhood to emerge. Some of the fears and challenges adolescent boys must face include:

- Leaving home and school, and accepting responsibility for self-reliance, self-support, financial and legal obligations.

- Setting one's own boundaries, making choices and decisions, and accepting responsibility for consequences.

- Dealing with the opposite sex, with relationships, sexual responsibility, and the emotional issues these entail (relating perhaps to potential rejection, insecurity, power struggles, roles, needs and expectations, jealousy, fidelity, commitment, and the grief and upheaval of endings).

- Taking responsibility for one's own mental and physical health, and making healthy, sensible adult choices.

- Having to speak one's own thoughts, learning to formulate and express adult opinions, and engage in discussion and negotiation of an adult standard.

- Being responsible for managing one's own emotions and emotional life, and meeting adult expectations of stability, communication, and conduct.

- Coping with the fear and anxiety of contending with and accommodating other people's difference – difference in culture, opinions, values, priorities, likes and dislikes; coping with the unknown in people and situations, and often having to encounter demands for which one's knowledge is inadequate.

- Commitment to long-term obligations, and the demands for self-discipline and perseverance.

- The responsibility of generativity: being no longer a mere dependant, but having to accept the adult male obligation of giving more than one takes, and being responsible not just for one's own, but also others' well-being and welfare.

- Coping with the self-consciousness, insecurities and anxieties of gaining acceptance, and achieving acceptable competence in the world of adults.

- Coping with the turmoil, change, confusion, loss and grief in relation to and amongst one's peers.

- Achieving some sense of a worthwhile and acceptable self-identity through, and in spite of, the turmoil of hormonal, physical, and body image changes, and the successes and failures entailed in adjusting and attaining to autonomous adult status.

- Dealing with the perplexing change in one's relationship with parents, and with any difficulties of parentalism or anxious tendencies of puerile regression.

- Daring to think and act as a man amongst men, in spite of feelings of inferiority, fears of rejection, and anxieties of comparable inexperience and perceived power-lessness.

A valuable tool for identifying fears and challenges worthy and needful of youthful engagement, is to identify the *goals* of behaviours - goals indicated by and often hidden behind behaviours. Behaviours have goals – goals we are not always aware of. Even highly negative behaviours often represent a person's attempt (however maladaptive, counterproductive or harmful) to meet a legitimate need – such as to feel noticed, accepted, safe, worthwhile, or to have a sense of personal agency, value or identity.

Identifying the goals of behaviours, and accepting the challenge of finding more appropriate behaviours for achieving them (should that be necessary), can be a powerfully transforming process – one that can contribute significantly to shaping mature personal responsibility and manliness.

Boys aspiring to manhood, and men, can also achieve both a sense of personal accomplishment and character development through the tests and rigours of physical activities and pursuits – particularly those set in or engaging the natural environment, such as hiking, climbing, sailing, canoeing, and the many forms of adventuring. Men will always feel the need for these activities, and society would do well to accommodate them. Certainly, risks need to be measured, along with the acquisition of requisite knowledge and skills, and the practice of thoughtful planning. But society will always need those prepared to test the limits of their physical and mental endurance and capacity; those with an adventurous spirit. Because such endeavours help keep alive and renew society's energy and optimism of human resourcefulness and indomitability; they help counter the potential paralysis of cynicism and pessimism, by engendering imagination, inspiration, and the faith that 'come what may', human will, ingenuity and character can always somehow win through.

Whatever the ordeals and testing boys and men may pass through, as has been customary in tribal societies, they must leave their mark – a mark that reminds of decision, changed orientation, new responsibility, and the commitment of the manly quest; a mark that can help maintain new manly consciousness. Rather than the scarring of cuts or absence of a tooth, such a mark may need be symbolised by something – perhaps something carried or worn. But the most important evidence and reinforcement of initiatory experience and transformation should be that exhibited in unarguable manliness – manly strength of virtue, and manly behaviour.

Instruction and Learning

Indispensable to the transformation and transition that initiatory experience aims to produce is *instruction* and *learning*. In traditional tribal societies this meant hearing about and perhaps seeing enacted the great myths of the tribe, and being instructed in the traditions, laws, and ways of tribal society and culture. All of this found great focus and intensity in the ritual place and 'sacred space' of the initiatory endeavour. But it is very difficult for men today to obtain instruction about what it means to be truly a man – to find a lucid profile of mature masculinity, a manhood ideal. Hence the purpose of our previous discussion about Reconstituting the Manhood Ideal (proposed as a starting point for the more comprehensive work that needs to be done in this area).

It is important to reiterate that instruction and learning pertaining to manliness is most potent in, and best suited to, the ritual place or 'sacred space' of men's gathering. Of course, there is much men can do as individuals (and in their mentoring of boys) to promote instruction, learning, and self-development, in order to aid the accomplishment of transformation and transition. Yet this also needs to occur in connection with and in the broad context of a supportive and validatory community of men.

Some key activities of instruction and learning include ordinary instruction and interactive learning, the use of myths, stories – and storytelling, invocation and archetypes, and encouraging the cultivation of the mind and reason.

There is an important role for simply instructing boys and men by expounding the attributes and meaning of the manhood ideal, and by promoting learning that is interactive, exploratory, and which engages personal stories and issues in an endeavour of 'applied man psychology'. As basic as this may sound, it is currently a rarity amongst Australian men. Yet it is foundational to any effort at reinstating neglected attributes of manhood, promoting an understanding of men's issues, honouring masculinity, and providing a focus for initiatory efforts.

Stories are a powerful and indispensable medium for instruction and learning. They are able to connect boys and men with the lineage of the male community, and deepen a sense of yearning for recognition and validation within it. In times past, sacred stories and myths were considered the greatest treasure anyone could possess:

> *Shamans were not judged by the things they owned, but by the stories they knew, the rituals they were authorised to conduct, the dances they could perform.*[38]

Storytellers were once greatly honoured as the repositories of stories containing all that was important to life.[39] There are many truths about life that can only be described or communicated in story or myth. When something like love can't be explained concretely, a story about someone who showed love can. Virtues like love, justice, courage, compassion and mercy demand to be illustrated.

As Wallace Clift points out:

> *Whatever values have grasped a people as the basic theme of and truths about life and about a response to life, have been set forth in a series of stories.*[40]

Men's gatherings can provide an opportunity for storytelling. Selected men can take the time to research and learn certain myths, legends and stories relevant for ennobling manhood and that can be told in gatherings. Ample resources are available for this from Celtic, Greek, and North American Indian mythologies – to name only several examples. Literature is available from major booksellers on how to use storytelling effectively.

Stories have the uncanny ability of being able to:

> *Connect us with a part of our psyches which has been abandoned by our culture, a part of us that is nourished by the infinite, the divine. We feel connected to the Otherness of the world when we feel the majesty and the mystery contained within millennia-old stories. We ask ourselves, why do*

> *these stories survive, and what do they have to teach us?* [41]

Just as it is important to instruction and learning, to hear the retelling of myths and stories – including those of recent history (such as from the Anzacs or the exploits of colonial explorers, adventurers and pioneers), it is vital that men have opportunity to tell their own stories. It can be greatly affirming, challenging, healing, transformative, and empowering for men to tell of, and take note of, significant aspects of their lives and experiences, through stories. As in psychotherapy, when a person has a safe opportunity to externalise their thoughts, feelings and experiences – and thereby discover new insight, sources of pride, and perhaps more positive or helpful ways of viewing their lives – so too, in telling their stories, men can retrieve forgotten resources and meaning, observe patterns and continuities, see new possibilities, and feel freshly challenged in their lives. Moreover, they can enrich, inform, and perhaps inspire others with their accounts, and create important windows onto reality for younger men.

In the process of dealing with everyday issues and events, all of us invoke images and thoughts in our minds (and 'mind's eye'). Not all of these are helpful. But regardless of whether they are helpful or not, they deeply affect our moods, attitudes, how we look at things, and what we do.

Invocation, or bringing to mind and focussing on an image or mental picture (of a kind that can 'speak' to us – or about which we can speak to ourselves), can be used consciously and deliberately in a way that is helpful to us. We can invoke images that symbolise attributes we want to experience and 'install' as part of our own repertoire of strengths and abilities.

For this, it is best to find an opportunity for quietness and privacy, in order to relax and clear one's mind. It is then possible to bring to mind a remembered image, or to focus on an actual image or picture – one that most powerfully bespeaks the patterning energy, ability or strength one needs to experience and assimilate.

Again, there is nothing uncommon or strange about this practice. It is comparable to what religions have always done, such as the use of icons in Greek and Russian Orthodoxy, and the images used in Catholicism. It is merely a more thoughtful, conscious, and positively oriented form of what each of us does in our minds and self-talk each day.

It may be useful to find a suitable image of one of the King, Warrior, Magician or Lover archetypes. For example, it may be that an aspect of personality that needs to be strengthened is that of *Warrior,* because one's work-life calls for greater courage, resolve, self-discipline, or loyalty and commitment to principle. Or it may be that one's capacity for empathy, compassion, sensitivity, deep feeling, or creativity needs to be extended or developed. For this an image of the *Lover* archetype may be valuable.

There is a limitless variety of effigies (including classic mythological and religious ones, and those of more recent personages) that may be useful. However, the meaning any image can have always comes from how it is perceived by an individual. What works for one person may not suit another.

Invocation, then, is simply finding and focussing on an image that is strongly symbolical of the energy, form and attributes that are needed to bring greater balance, strength, and integrity to one's capacity for manliness.

As was noted earlier, Neojungians emphasise how meditating on archetypal images can not only deepen an awareness of the nature of archetypes, but can invite their transformative patterning power into human experience.

There is a whole tradition in Britain of groups and societies using the Arthurian archetypes in this way. Arthurian scholar, John Matthews, gives a first-hand account of being present at and participating in a group working with these archetypes:

> *The prophecy of the return of Arthur was fulfilled that night at the Camelot we had built. After reading of Tennyson's Morte d'Arthur, we invited back into our company the redeemed archetypes of the Round Table. We sat silently, for what seemed an age, invoking the personages with whom we had become so familiar throughout the weekend, sending them forth to intercede with the troubled world of our times. It was truly an awesome and splendid thing that we did. The power we invoked was both visible and perceptible in every sense. None of us wanted to leave: we were gripped, not by fear, but by a longing to remain. Then one by one the company dispersed to bear into the world the substance of what we had experienced, to continue the work of the Round Table in our own sphere of life.*[42]

Another activity within the compass of instruction and learning, vital to effective transformation and transition, is the cultivation of mind and reason. Though this obviously cannot be accomplished in an 'experiential instant', making the transition from thinking and reasoning as a boy/child to thinking and reasoning as a man/adult is essential to manliness.

A man must 'know his own mind', not just know someone else's, or be carried along by unreasoning prejudice or an ideology. It is needful for him to: develop informed opinions about important issues, and beliefs based on refined knowledge, confirmed wisdom, and experience; form values informed by sacred and ancient sources, and the realities of contemporary experience and life.

This doesn't require higher education – it requires the formative influence of mature manhood and the encouragement of mature men. It also requires a commitment to responsibility – for one's own mental life, and for what good this can contribute to communal life.

Unfortunately, as Oscar Wilde observed,

> *Most people are other people. Their thoughts are someone else's opinions, their lives a mimicry, their passions a quotation.*[43]

Knowing his own mind, and having the openness and humility to acknowledge and utilise the wisdom and knowledge of others (and 'becoming artful in gleaning the truthful core in views of every kind'[44]), provides a man with crucial stimuli of moral consciousness, and a basis for sound decision making and action.

Consolidation and Return

Whatever change and transformation boys and men may attain through use of initiatory means (whether in a collective ritual or personal endeavour), such gains will need to be 'cemented' as best they can, and taken back and applied in everyday life. But we should not be naïve about the difficulties this may entail. In an ideological and cultural climate that does not warm to the idea of a resurgent masculinity (in any form), and with the still prevalent emphases on men as abusers, patriarchal oppressors, less than competent fathers and husbands, and persons deficient in the conduct of their emotions, men's enthusiasm and good intentions can be all too easily dashed by others' hostility, cynicism, or disinterest. This also highlights how needful is the support of a community of like-minded men, and a capacity for 'standing on solid ground' within one's own sense of manhood.

Another idea to consider is that many people (including young people) feel impotent in modern society and alienated from the world order around them – perhaps, as Joseph Campbell suggests, due to a:

> *Stagnation of inauthentic lives and living that has settled upon us...that evokes nothing of our spiritual life, our potentialities or even our physical courage...*[45]

In this setting, notions of moral consciousness, character, virtue, a manhood ideal, or initiatory process, may seem quite foreign, archaic, or 'religious', and may consequently not always meet with a positive reception.

At the best of times it can be difficult to hold onto and apply a newly acquired consciousness, insight or experience, much like Western travellers who journey to a third world country, experience a profound shift in outlook, and vow to apply this on returning home, but often never quite manage to do so. Consolidating and applying initiatory experience will (just as in the case of traditional tribal societies) need to be bolstered by both the support of other men, and a continuous process of reinforcement and enhancement through grounding in the manhood ideal and the self-rewarding *practice* of manliness.

Practising manliness often calls for the discipline of a purposive act of will. We may not at first feel like the person we want to be, or feel like doing what needs to be done. Like an actor who decides to 'get into character', we may only begin to feel like the character once we have started to act like him – moving, talking, behaving like him. A man that does not feel he has inner strength, resolve, or courage, may need to start behaving as if he does, until some accomplishment confirms with feelings that indeed he does, and like this he is. Likewise, a man may not feel sensitive or compassionate, though manliness calls for these attributes. He may need to put himself in circumstances that 'bring these out in him'; he will have only to genuinely act with sensitivity and compassion, to begin to know something of the feeling of being a sensitive and compassionate person.

A more complete sense of who we are and what we may be as men can only derive from our concrete actions – especially those that are self-giving and focussed on the needs not just of ourselves but of others. Out of a given life can emerge a new life.

One further important consideration here is that of mentors and mentoring (a topic to be discussed more fully shortly). A very effective way of consolidating and enhancing the gains of initiatory experience is by accepting responsibility for being an example and encouragement to those less experienced or those as yet uninitiated. Young men (within the capacity of their experience and maturity), and older mature men, can both assist boys aspiring to be men in their initiatory endeavour. And both (though mostly older men) may provide ongoing mentoring, and a point of reference within a community of men, for boys and young men at various stages and through the various experiences of their development.

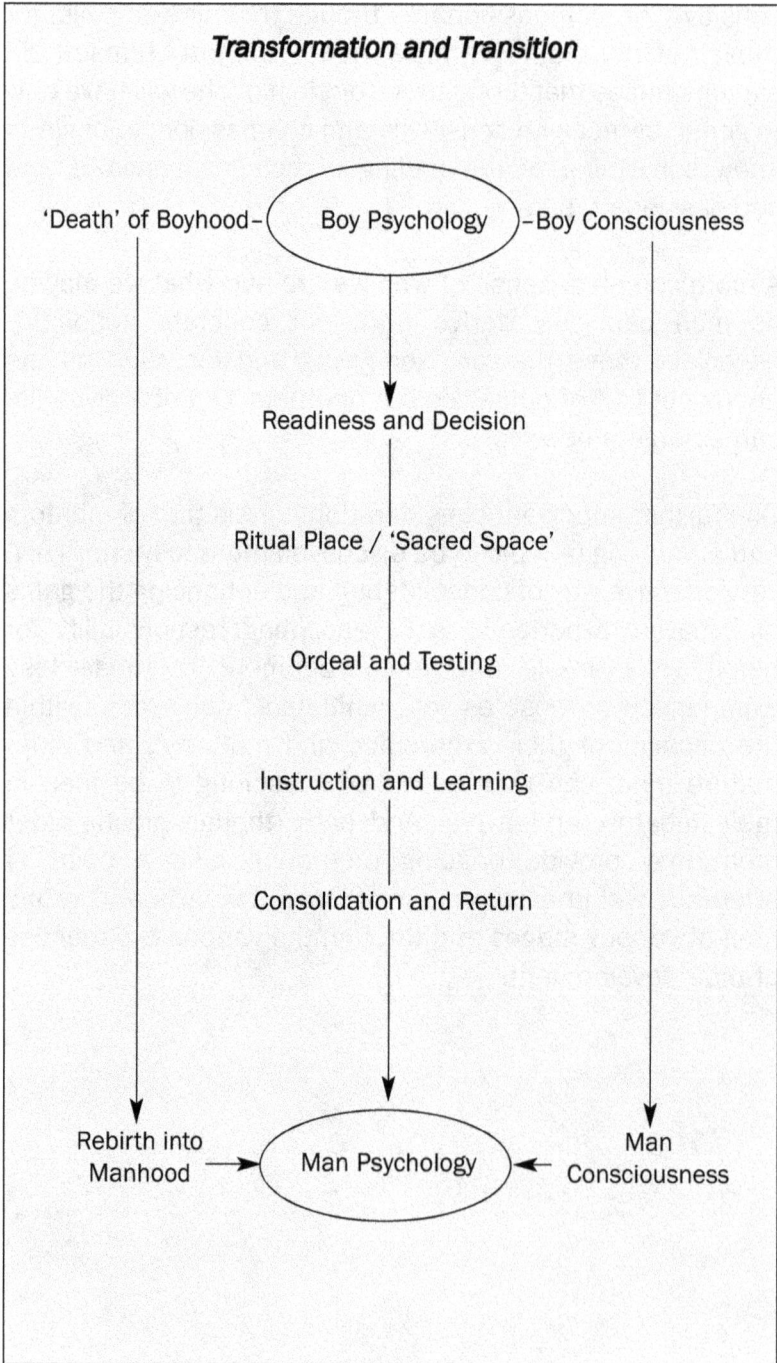

Transformation and Transition

'Death' of Boyhood – Boy Psychology – Boy Consciousness

Readiness and Decision

Ritual Place / 'Sacred Space'

Ordeal and Testing

Instruction and Learning

Consolidation and Return

Rebirth into Manhood → Man Psychology ← Man Consciousness

Table 16

THE ROLE AND IMPORTANCE OF MENTORS

There now exists a comprehensive literature on the subject of mentoring, so the purpose here will be merely to highlight some key observations about the important role of male mentors.

Mentor, in Homer's *The Odyssey*, was the friend to whom Ulysses, in his absence, entrusted his son Telemachus. Mentor was to provide him with wise counsel and guidance. Hence the meaning of *mentor* in modern usage, which refers to one who acts as a role model, confidant, advisor, advocate, and companion, to a younger less experienced person.

Mentoring is gaining increasing popularity in Western countries, especially as an effective preventative strategy with adolescent boys at risk. But it is also recognised as one of the best known ways of improving outcomes for male adolescents, who must not only deal with the upheaval of change in their bodies, their sense of self, and their relationships with peers, siblings, parents and teachers, but must face the immense challenge of readying themselves for manhood.[46/47]

Interactions within families at this time, and attempts at discussing and working through the issues of all these changes, are commonly difficult and fraught with potential conflict and misunderstanding.

Being the parent of a child approaching adulthood, balancing caring with trying to ensure that a child is sufficiently encouraged and supported in their need and endeavour to grow up, is no easy thing. With the best of intentions, fathers and their sons can all too easily get caught up in an escalating 'battle of wills', in a pattern of overreacting and recrimination, mutual frustration and avoidance. Only in recent times has any society had the expectation that a boy's biological father was the natural person to assist with his process of initiation into the world of men and manly responsibilities. Most commonly in traditional cultures, the mother's brother would fulfil this role.[48]

As Joseph Palmour points out:

> *A father's gifts, calling, or education might make him totally unfit to initiate his own son into the discipline, the wisdom, and the personal relationships that would perfect a boy with radically different needs than his own. There is simply nothing to prevent a deeply intellectual father, for example, from having a highly athletic, non-contemplative son, and vice versa. An aggressive, bullish father can have a sensitive, artistic son.*[49]

It appears needful for our society – particularly because of its complexity and ever increasing demand for specialised roles, that we take a lesson from traditional societies, which obviously 'grasped the practical importance of such a lack of fit between father and son'.[50]

As foreign as it may sound to many fathers today, their most caring and responsible act of fathering may be to recognise the limitations of what they can do to help their sons in their most critical time of growing up, and to put effort into finding someone else better suited to giving them what they need. We need to affirm fathers that can show this maturity of responsibility, relieving them of any guilt from the illusion that somehow they must furnish all that is needed for their son's wellbeing and adult development. It may well be that a father could more naturally mentor another man's son, rather than his own. And how much better would it be if a father could:

> *...proudly help his son find a man or men who will initiate him into a discipline and wisdom which might be different from that which the father has himself.*[51]

The role of a mentor is not as a replacement father, or as a surrogate parent, but is that of a mature manly role model and friend, who can help a young male have confidence in himself, see the options available to him, define himself in an appropriate way, experience a yearning to be the best of which he is capable, and to attain to honourable manliness.

Even with supportive parents, many young males become cynical and apathetic about their prospects and future; they struggle to find worthwhile values and goals, and even more to see value in themselves – largely because they lack the essential underpinning and support of being meaningfully connected with older men whom they can respect and trust.

A young male struggling with the whole process of becoming a man can benefit little from what many well-meaning women might say to him in encouragement. And yet one small genuine affirmation from a respected older man may prove sustenance enough for years of self-belief and indomitable effort. 'He said I could, from then on I knew I could!' Moore and Gillette have argued that, above all:

> *Young men today are starving for blessing from older men. They need to be blessed... because if they are, something inside will come together for them. That is the effect of blessing; it heals and makes whole.*[52]

What does it take to be a mentor? Well it doesn't depend on education, status, or occupation. It's more about experience, authenticity, depth of character and caring.[53]

We could begin to make a list of the kind of qualities needful in a mentor by perhaps thinking back across our own lives – by remembering the people that influenced us in some way; that played some important role. Maybe they helped us choose a path we took or a decision we made; or they made a real difference to the way we felt about things because of something they said or did – something small to them (maybe of which they were unaware), but important to us. Perhaps what was most memorable was that someone took an interest in us, really listened, or sowed some seeds of encouragement, confidence or accomplishment in us. Perhaps most profoundly, at a time when we felt least worthwhile (maybe because of our acting out, and other peoples' negative reactions), someone showed they accepted us as we were, believed in us, and cared about what happened to us. When a man does that for a boy, he may have changed his whole life without knowing it.

The importance of mentoring is not just its potential benefits for those mentored. Mentors themselves benefit significantly. Joseph Palmour suggests that mentoring can unlock a whole lot of 'dammed-up energy' inside men. And that older men – particularly at mid-life will:

> ...stagnate if they don't learn to reach out to the young in friendship rather than feeling contemptuously superior toward them. A more generative interest in young people can help men in their prime regain a sense of moral initiative in their lives and overcome a gnawing sense of guilt for having neglected their thoughtful idealism. The admiration of younger men can inspire them to live up to the same values and standards they encourage in their protégés... Mentoring is thus a natural bridge between generations that can be greatly fulfilling to each.[54/55]

The importance of the role of mentor cannot be overstressed, because it is not only beneficial to those who are the immediate recipients of its effects, but is vital to the whole endeavour of reinstating the neglected attributes of manliness, and to reclaiming the initiative in ensuring appropriate opportunities and conditions for the socialisation of boys.

The Role of Male Mentor	
He is a:	Role Model
	Confidant
	Advisor
	Advocate
	Companion/Friend
He:	Listens
	Cares
	Encourages
	Shows Empathy
	Is non-judgemental
	Is accepting
	Builds self-belief, self-worth and self-confidence
	Helps with problem-solving and goal setting
	Provides a connection with the wider community of men
	Helps to identify and develop strengths, abilities, and gifts
	Helps to envisage possibilities and identify opportunities
He is not:	A surrogate parent
	A substitute father
	An authoritarian
	A social worker
	A rescuer
	A dictator

Table 17

MEN'S WORK IN THE AUSTRALIAN SETTING

Here we will consider briefly some of the historical cultural influences that have helped shape Australian manhood – influences that have also served to produce certain cultural codes that remain an influential dimension of our fundamental Australian cultural identity and disposition. These observations can not only provide us with some basic insights into how the general notion of manhood in Australia needs to be reconstituted – to be brought into balance; but also by what other means work with men and boys – and a legitimate and effective men's movement – can be furthered, relative to the Australia cultural disposition.

Australian Mythologies

A number of writers have sought to identify what is exceptional and distinctive about the Australian cultural identity and character. Donald Horne (1964), Russell Ward (1958), Arthur Phillips (1958), and Craig McGregor (1968), have provided much insight into Australian mythologies. These mythologies are most familiar to us through their iconic representations of the 'Australian man': the larrikin, bushranger, swagman, rural battler, pioneer, gold miner/frontiersman, and Anzac.

The mythologies behind these representations are some of the historic formative influences on, and arguably contain some of the chief constituents of, contemporary Australian manhood. Just as importantly, they continue to be some of the fundamental underpinnings of our national character and psyche, in the form of 'dominant cultural codes of popular solidarity'.[56]

Such myths are the means by which we try to explain who we are, how we have become who we are, why we behave the way we do, and how we should behave. Here it will suffice to make comment on how these myths arose and the kind of messages they have conveyed.

Convict heritage

The mythology of our convict heritage is a colourful one. The convict beginnings of white Australia were most conspicuously violent beginnings. As historian Russell Ward has pointed out:

> *For nearly the first half century of its existence, white Australia was primarily an extensive gaol... convict influence on Australian society was very much more important than has usually been supposed.*[57]

In fact, over 70 years after the first fleet and the start of the gold rushes, still the majority of the population were convict related.[58] A part of the convict myth is that convicts were mainly innocent victims of a British class system. Most were actually habitual criminals, whose crimes did arise out of poverty and the need to survive it.[59] But what were the effects on later society of this convict past? Well it doesn't appear to have made Australians criminally inclined, but it did produce a resentment and suspicion of authority, and a society that gave far less credence to class distinctions than in England.[60]

The Australian bush

When the first settlers arrived in Australia, all was 'bush' – vast, wild, and unforgiving land; a sunburnt country prone to drought, floods and bushfires. For much of the first part of the century, the economy was based on farming bush land. Surviving these harsh conditions necessitated cooperation. With the discovery of gold and other metals, mining 'outback' – as well as farming and pastoral activities, provided much of Australia's wealth.[61] Though even by 1901 the majority of Australians lived in coastal regions rather than the far outback, the psychological legacy of the bush remains within the Australian psyche and cultural identity.[62]

A number of characteristics attributed to Australians derive from the lives of the early bush workers, and emanate from accounts of bushrangers like Ned Kelly, the men of the gold rush (many of whom were labourers who deserted their masters for the diggings), and the Eureka Stockade. These characteristics include a dislike for authority, fierce independence (doing things one's own way), practicality, an unpretentious manner, hospitality, and (from bushrangers and rebel miners) a preparedness to be an antiauthoritarian champion of the underdog, and to fight a corrupt establishment.[63]

It is important to note here the difference between 'the frontier' of Australia compared to that of America. 'Both have histories of war between white invaders and indigenous inhabitants, of farms hewn out of hard earth, of towns that gradually become "civilized" instead of "outback", of class struggle between land barons and workers.'[64] But, as Ward points out, these frontiers and their early frontiersmen gave rise to different kinds of societies. The American landscape could sustain small holdings. The Australian frontier required mostly larger acreages to sustain economic farming – which often required more than just a family – shepherds, stockman and other workers were needed. The necessities of survival and harsh frontier conditions fostered group solidarity, loyalty, and 'pulling together' – the qualities summed up in 'mateship'.[65]

The idea of mateship was perhaps most pronounced in the early part of our history. The great Australian author Henry Lawson refers to the idea of mateship frequently in his writings. It is a term that was significant in the trenches of World War 1 and the Anzacs. The story of Simpson, the brave ambulance man who collected his wounded comrades with a donkey and returned them to the safety of the trenches, is a powerful symbol of Australian mateship.[66]

The Anzacs (referring to the Australian and New Zealand Army Corps)
Of all the Australian myths, that of the Anzacs is perhaps most well known; celebrated yearly throughout Australia with memorials in almost every town and city. In recent times its telling and celebration have actually increased in popularity; it undoubtedly 'stands tall and proud' within the Australian cultural identity. In fact thousands of young Australians travel to the place of the most famous ANZAC military campaign of the First World War, fought against the Turks at Gallipoli.

The myth of the Anzacs, as with that of the bush, not only gave rise to the idea of mateship, but also antiauthoritarianism. The diggers found it repugnant to defer to officers in the manner that the British soldiers did. British officers were viewed as snobbish and tyrannical incompetents.[67] But the Anzac myth is also a myth of male bonding, heroism, and egalitarianism. An Australian calls no man his master. In these respects the ANZAC and bush myths are quite closely related.[68]

There is a shadow side here that must also be noted. Historian, Martin Crotty, has pointed out:

> Militarist and nationalist constructions of manliness reached their logical culmination in the idolisation of the Anzac soldier... although the sight of young men inculcated to believe in the qualities of heroism and self-sacrifice appealed to contemporaries, and although this vision still dominates popular memory of the Anzac experience, it needs to be remembered that it resulted in often futile slaughter on the slopes of Gallipoli and in the mud of the Western Front.[69]

The strength of this idealisation quickly waned with the 'spectacle of shattered veterans returning home, and the absence of those who did not return at all'.[70] The tragedy of this period of the early twentieth century is that qualities of discipline, loyalty and athleticism were harnessed in destructive ways (precisely the problem discussed in an earlier chapter concerning an unbalanced manhood ideal). A tragedy also was that this 'was all but impervious to those voices which dared to question it'.[71]

Have we since achieved some balance in our expectations and emphases of manhood? Crotty suggests that significant change has occurred, and that the 'most violent, anti-intellectual, and virulently racist and sexist elements of what used to be the "centre" are now firmly confined to the margins'.[72] Nevertheless, strong resonances of the past do remain; emphases of brawn, 'bravery' and athleticism still tend to overshadow intelligence, sensitivity, humanness and other essential masculine attributes in popular Australian culture.

Despite this 'mixed bag' which is the legacy of our early history, the Anzac and other Australian mythologies have furnished our cultural identity with many robust and potentially meaningful elements (see Table 18).

Men's Work and the Australian Cultural Disposition

Though we need to be cautious about trying to attribute too much to the influence of these mythologies in contemporary Australian society, they have undoubtedly significantly contributed to the shaping of Australian manhood and our general cultural disposition.

For our purposes these observations provide us with a useful general profile of manhood in Australia which, though far from comprehensive, does suggest some very obvious ways in which we must endeavour (as already discussed at length) to bring balance and integrity to the manhood ideal. It is also important for us to take note of the apparent amenabilities suggested by our general

Manhood Characteristics and Cultural Codes Reflected in Australian Mythologies	
Companionate mateship	Group solidarity
Personal Autonomy	Fierce independence
Doing things one's own way	Personal initiative
Call no man master	Egalitarianism
Loyalty	Hospitality
Stands up for the underdog	Fights corrupt establishment
Committed to a 'fair go'	Values fairness and equity
Bravery	Self-Sacrifice
Discipline	Athleticism
Suspicious of hierarchy	
Views illegitimate authority and class distinctions with disdain	

Table 18

cultural disposition – reflected in male oriented activities and programs that are occurring unapologetically and with official authorisation. At least initially, this may indicate some of the most opportune strategic directions for a men's movement in Australia.

It would appear to be the case that the particular politicising influence of historic Australian mythologies on the Australian disposition has produced a concern with fairness, opposition to institutional behaviour that is oppressive, and a tendency to 'rise to the occasion' when an injustice becomes clearly evident. The 'underdog', even though not faultless, is deemed deserving of concerted support (a social reflex not lost on party political campaigners!). This disposition may help explain our current social amenability which is permitting (despite contrary ideological currents) the emergence of a 'movement' emphasising the needs and issues of men and boys (as no less legitimate than those of women and girls). This bid for gender equity is in evidence in the health and human service sectors,[73/74] and in public education.[75/76] There is also currently much public discussion about the equity of access, custody and shared parenting provisions relative to separated fathers,[77] and political support for much recent advertising asserting the positive role of fathers.[78]

This amenability may bode well for the furtherance of a men's movement in Australia, if such a movement can advance intelligently argued alternatives to the profeminist status quo. In North America it would appear that men's movements are either predominantly profeminist or mythopoetic in their approach. The latter movement, whilst laudible in its work in promoting personal development and male rapport, has failed to adequately critique or challenge the profeminist monopoly in influencing public and institutional perceptions on gender issues. Nor has it developed an alternative and viable political/theoretical position on gender, capable of mounting such a challenge.[79]

In Australia such an entrenched and polarised situation does not yet exist. And perhaps given our cultural disposition, which appears to be amenable to reason on the grounds of fairness, justice and equity, there may be potential for a quite different outcome – if men can mobilise to formulate a viable alternative approach to the questions of gender, masculinity and manhood; an approach that deals intelligently with available data both from research and the lived reality of peoples lives.

Australian men may not generally or easily take themselves off to join groups that are 'feel-good', or are promoting mutual nurture and bonding. However they may be responsive to being mobilised by the injustices of certain gender inequities, and, in the process, rediscover and experience the immense personal benefits that a purposeful community and solidarity of men can provide.

Another example of an apparent amenability of our particular Australian cultural disposition (based on a strong ethic of companionate mateship, and a valuing of individuality) is evident in the emergence and popularity of mentoring programs. Though this is still only a fledgling phenomenon, it has been well supported by government and communities across Australia.[80] There is little question that mentoring – particularly for young males, holds immense potential for improved socialisation, and assisting them in their difficult transition from boy psychology to man psychology – from boyhood to responsible adulthood.[81]

Of course mentoring is also popular in America; however, perhaps a particular quality of mentoring will be achieved in the Australian setting – one that is not so much success focussed (underpinned by the American cultural mythology of 'rags to riches') as one that encourages whatever kind of individuality or 'being your own man' that the benefits of mateship and someone 'looking out for you' can produce; contrasting the American mythology with the ideas of sufficiency, personal freedom, autonomy, and doing things one's own way.

Akin to mentoring, as an example that may reflect a certain cultural amenability, is the popularity and success of 'Men's Shed' projects across Australia. These projects have been found to fit very comfortably with male notions of mateship, group solidarity, personal initiative, practicality, and hospitality.[82] Such projects not only bring together men of a variety of ages and backgrounds in activities such as metalwork, woodwork, working on mechanical tasks, and welding, but they are also invaluable vehicles for promoting social, physical and mental health.

Perhaps the biggest challenge for the furtherance of work with men and boys, and a meaningful men's movement in Australia, remains the contaminating legacy of gender feminism. Few projects and programs for men and boys appear to be able to fully break free of this pervasive male-devaluing ideology – simply because there is too little information and so few printed resources available to equip and inform them otherwise. Though there is no shortage of male exponents of profeminism, it is highly unlikely that this ideology would succeed with men if they had access to a sound and explanatory alternative – a better way of understanding gender, gender relations, men and men's issues.

There is a great need for an entirely new approach to these concerns, and one that can be made widely available to inform the many currently emerging initiatives intended (or at least ostensibly intended) to benefit men and boys. Such an approach needs to be affirmative, equitable, intellectually tenable, and one that abstains from any semblance of the prevailing tendency to reinforce a deficit image of men.*

---

* This present volume, and a previous one, *The Making of a Man: Recovering masculinity and manhood in the light of reason*[83] are intended as a contribution to this endeavor.

What has been said thus far about cultural amenabilities should not be taken to suggest that the furtherance of work with men and boys, or a men's movement in Australia, is dependent on accommodation to traits of cultural disposition. The advancement of this work is first and foremost a radical endeavour, one concerned with a new vision of manhood and gender relations. It will necessitate a recasting of some behavioural conventions with which men have become comfortable. Because whatever the notional appeal or resonance the more refined attributes of manhood may have with men, their realisation will demand overcoming awkwardness, experiencing new vulnerabilities, practising new roles, learning to negotiate and work with moral concepts, and personal and group processes of ethical reasoning. All of this will be necessary if purposeful, intentional male gatherings and male 'community' are to be an adequate and supportive context in which men can give expression to emotion, formulate and practice initiatory process, and constitute a primary vehicle both for socialisation and for exemplary social action.

To conclude our discussion of *men's work in the Australian setting*, it may be useful to briefly explore the needful emphases and/or changes in social policy, and some useful vehicles or processes of socialization that might serve to enhance work with men and boys, and progress a legitimate men's movement. Though space here permits only a cursory treatment of these topics, they are clearly needful of much further attention and detailed research.

Social Policies

Of crucial importance to permitting and promoting important work with men and boys, and the progress of a men's movement, will be a particular focus on social policy: seeking to ensure that social policies reflect the accountability and responsibilities that government must exercise in relation to all society's constituent members – male and female. Chief amongst these responsibilities is not only to strive to maintain order and viable economy, but also to ensure in all its functions that it is equitable – fair and just.

By insisting on equity, there is much scope to draw away from glib and often contradictory generalisations of equality (largely premised on the untenable dogma of gender interchangeability), and instead to highlight and value the obvious differences in the kinds of issues, needs, abilities, preferences and capacities that men and women generally have. To take health policy, for example, for it to be equitable it should reflect known differences between men's and women's sex–specific psychology and physiology, their characteristic help-seeking behaviours, their particular issues of access and preferences of service delivery settings and methods, and, of course, their known comparable health status.

It is all too easy to blame men for their low attendance at health clinics, poor health choices, and (compared to women) very poor general health status. And yet (as already alluded to in the chapter *Men and Emotions*), so-called 'mainstream' services are largely perceived by men as male unfriendly and often inappropriate in nature, location, accessibility and convenience.

In social policies relating to welfare, insisting on gender equity would suggest the need for a wider-ranging review of the assumptions, methods, attitudes, and funding priorities of many agencies and services, which, in areas like counselling, emergency accommodation, and parent support (to name only a few), have failed to understand and take account of men's and boy's gender specific needs and issues.

These and all other domains of social policy need to be lobbied to demonstrate gender equity in their resource allocation and service delivery priorities and methods. The strategic plans and statements of principle of public sector and almost all private sector institutions concerned with health, welfare, and social issues, incorporate obligations of equity. The challenge ahead is to make such institutions and agencies accountable for the *practise* of equity, by subjecting their priorities and practices to scrutiny, along with informing them about specifically what gender equity requires – particularly for men and boys.

A pragmatic point that should not be overlooked in any endeavour to make public institutions (and most charitably funded private ones) genuinely gender equitable, is that women *and* men finance such endeavours (whether by their taxes or donations), and therefore both can rightly demand policies and expenditures that are fair, just, and responsive to their particular issues and needs. It is high time we ceased to permit partisan gender ideology to influence these determinations.

If we ensure that social policies incorporate gender equity provisions relative to the demonstrable needs, issues, health and well being status of women and men, there is potential to create a number of wide-ranging and important effects – beyond those of improved services for men and boys.

Institutions and agencies compelled to demonstrate gender equity in the way they operate would have much need of information and education in order to both understand and respond to the gender-specific needs of men and boys. This would have the effect of making necessary a whole raft of ongoing in-service training initiatives for health, welfare, and human service workers. It would also require tertiary training institutions (such as the Universities and TAFE

Colleges) to provide subjects, courses and program options that must move beyond the indefensible and inequitable gender bias of conventional male-diminishing dogma. Such requirements of education and training, and education and training reform, would require that capable men exercise leadership in informing, guiding and evaluating these processes. This would provide much needed opportunities for reforming not only the current offerings of education providers, but also the cultures and attitudes of major institutions (governed by social policies), and, in turn, the way they influence the perceptions and attitudes of wider society concerning gender issues. Even moderate changes of this kind would doubtless provide immense scope and demand for work with men and boys, and the legitimisation and need of a sound, resourceful, and society-nurturing men's movement.

Perhaps a no more important example of the need for policy reform and accountability to constituents for genuine gender equity is in our school system.

With the advent of state sponsored and authorised political correctness, positive discrimination, and male diminishing ideology and methodology in our schools, we are lately bemoaning the unhappiness, uncontrollability and poor academic performance of boys at school. There is simply no disputing that our school system is now failing boys, just as it once failed girls (though in quite different ways). Whether measured by academic or psycho–social criteria, we are doing damage to the lives of a whole generation of future men.[84/85]

Fortunately there is a growing interest in what is happening for boys in education, evidenced in much recent media coverage and in the debates and discussion occurring within education departments and the academe.[86/87] As with other areas of social policy, the degree to which education policy can be made to reflect the principle and requirement of authentic gender equity (rather than a glib notion of equality dressed up as equity), of a kind that takes account of empirical evidence about on-average sex-specific differences in aptitudes, behaviours, needs, issues, and interests, the school system itself will need reorientating and re-educating. Not only will boys (who are 'men in the making') benefit hugely by progress in this area, but so will the whole endeavour of legitimising and furthering work with men and boys, and a men's movement.

Vehicles/Processes of Socialization

In previous chapters much has already been said about the need for improvements in the way we socialize boys, and the potential difficulties they experience in the absence of adequate mature male support and facilitation in the transition and transformation needed to achieve successful adulthood.

The value of a 'community of men' and all-male environments and activities, which can also have a thoughtful and considered focus on the psychosocial needs and issues of boys, cannot be over-emphasised.

It has also been noted that significant opportunities are available for improved socialization of boys in the practise of mentoring, and by creating ritual and instructive accompaniments (based on the attributes of a reconstituted manhood ideal) for the various markers of adult age and responsibility – such as attaining voting age, or 21 years of age (traditionally celebrated as a 'coming of age').

Some promising new vehicles for socialization are in the form of interactive educative group programs currently being run in some South Australian schools. These programs focus directly on what it means to be a man, and seek to differentiate between boy and man psychology by using a range of situational scenarios, behavioural choices, and ethical dilemmas. Titled *Straight Talking* and *Talking to Boys about Being Men*, these programs have been eagerly taken up by primary and secondary schools, and propose an excellent strategy for Australia-wide use.[88]

Linked to this strategy, training for parents and teachers on how to more effectively respond to the particular developmental and psychosocial needs and issues of boys (including behavioural issues), suggests a potent combination of means for reorientating and enhancing the capacity of the two most influential contexts and vehicles of socialisation – home and school.[89/90]

There is much untapped potential in the popular 'Men's Shed' programs. Though most of these have been funded and set up to cater for veterans and older men, they could (with appropriate support and training), be enabled to provide an invaluable environment for boys to engage in practical activities and skill development under the guidance of older men, and in an all-male environment.

Carefully selected mature men in these programs – if trained and adequately supported, could also serve as reliable location based mentors and confidants for boys.

Despite the recent notoriety of some sporting clubs and organisations due to the anti-social (and sometimes allegedly criminal) behaviour of some of their members, there is much potential for sporting bodies to become vehicles of appropriate male socialization. They could be offered educative programs (for training coaches and/or directly for players) designed to foster mature and responsible male behaviour, and to encourage new standards of conduct.

It may be possible to work with some organisations to adopt a whole new ethic and sense of responsibility for providing the setting, structure, programs and incentives, and rewards, for promoting male maturation and the formation of character. It is hard to imagine how this would do anything other than attract strong community support, and achieve a much enhanced and rewarding public image.

Finally, there are many activities that can be specifically organised by mature men that can create ample opportunity for meaningfully engaging boys in experiences formative of character. Whether the 'rough and tumble' of outdoors adventure and endurance (much suited to Australia's extensive natural and wilderness resources), or more group interactive ideas/communication based activities, the only limitations are imagination and the initiative of concerned men. The latter must become a matter of central concern to any legitimate men's movement, which must, above all, help men recover faith in themselves, the moral authority and responsibility of mature manliness, and the confidence and resolve to reclaim their vital masculine role within society.

References

1. Moore, R. and Gillette, D., **King, Warrior, Magician, Lover: Recovering The archetypes of The Mature Masculine** (U.S.A., Harper Collins, 1990) p. 7

2. Ibid., Introduction, p. xvii

3. Based on the author's work with men and men's groups over a fifteen year period, including specific discussions about leadership, character, and personal change

4. Turner, V., **The Ritual Process** (Ithaca, New York, Cornell university Press, 1969)

5. Eliade, M., **Birth and Rebirth** (New York, Harper and Row, 1958)

6. Campbell, J., **The Power of Myth** (London, Anchor Books, 1988) p. 9

7. Op. cit., Moore & Gillette, p. 6

8. Eliade, M., **Rites and Symbols of Initiation: The Mysteries of Birth and Rebirth** (U.S.A., Spring Publications, 1994)

9. Turner, P., **The Double Meaning of Initiation In Theological Expression** *in* Imaginer La théologie catholique, Permanance et transformations de la foi en attendant Jésus-Christ: Mélanges offerts à Ghislain Lafont. Jeremy Driscoll (ed.) (Studia Anselmaiana 129 Rome, Centro Studi Sant' Anselmo, 2000) pp. 487-499

10. Op. cit., Eliade, 1994

11. **Rites of Initiations** (South African Veterans Assoc. 1997) Available online – http://w1.864.telia.com./~u86437531/p26.htm

12. Op. cit., Turner, 1969

13. Hoitt, A., **The Native Tribes of South-East Australia** (London, 1904), pp. 628-631 Available online – http://alexm.here.ru/mirrors/www.enteract.com/jwalz/Eliade/142.html

14. Op. cit., Campbell, 1988, pp. 101 & 102

15. **Australia: Secrets of The Dreamtime** *in* **Goodbye To Innocence: The Making of An Adult**. *New Internationalist,* 138, August 1984

16. Op. cit., Eliade, 1994

17. Gilmore, D., **Manhood In the Making: Cultural Concepts of Masculinity** (U.S.A., Yale University Press, 1990) chapter 6, pp. 123-145

18. Ibid.

19. **Nepal: The Fall of The Goddess** *in* **Goodbye to Innocence: The Making of An Adult**. *New Internationalist*, 138, August, 1984

20. Op. cit., Campbell, 1988, p. 157

21. Campbell, J., **The Hero With A Thousand Faces** (U.S.A., Princeton University Press, 1972)

22. Animas Valley Institute, **Vision Quest** Available online http://www.animas.org/2003_animas_quest.htm

23. Op. cit., Campbell, 1988, pp.157 & 158

24. Op. cit., Animas Valley Institute

25. Ibid.

26. Op. cit., Moore & Gillette, p. 45

27. Op. cit., Campbell, 1988, p. 178

28. Emerson, R.W., **The Journals and Miscellaneous Notebooks of Ralph Waldo Emerson,** Sealts, M. (ed.) (U.S.A., Harvard university Press, 1965) Vol. 5, p. 38

29. Hillman, J., **The Soul's Code: In Search of Character and Calling** (Australian, Random House, 1996) p. 63

30. Ibid., p. 77

31. Ibid., p. 86

32. **Hamlyn Encyclopedic World Dictionary** (London, Hamlyn Publishing, 1971) p. 1760

33. Harvey, A., **A Journey In Ladakh** (London, Picador, 1993) p. 15

34. Fox, M., **Breakthrough: Meister Eckhart's Creation Spirituality In New Translation** (U.S.A., Image Books, 1980) p.241

35. See: Egan, H., **Christian Mysticism: The Future of a Tradition** (U.S.A., Pueblo Publishing, 1984)

36. Bridges, W., **Transitions: Making Sense of Life's Changes** (U.S.A., Addision-Wesley Publishing Co., 1980) p. 5

37. Horace, **'To Lollius'** *in* **Epistles** Book 1, 2.

38. Maddern, R., **A Teachers Guide To Storytelling At Historic Sites** (date and publisher unknown) p. 5

39. Ibid.

40. Clift, W., **Jung and Christianity: The Challenge of Reconciliation** (Australia, Collins-Dove, 1989) p. 69

41. Taylor, G., **Why Use Myths and Fairy Tales?** *in* **Wingspan: Inside The Men's Movement** Harding, C. (ed.) (New York, Saint Martins Press, 1992) p. 122

42. Matthews, J., **The Arthurian Tradition** (U.K., Element Books, 1994) p. 85

43. Oscar Wilde, **De Profundis** *in* **The Merriam Webster Dictionary of Quotations,** 1992, p. 217

44. Bishop Dom Helder Camara (published source unknown)

45. Op. cit., Campbell, 1988, p. 161

46. Rhodes, J., **Stand By Me: The Risks and Rewards of Mentoring Today's Youth** (U.S.A., Harvard University Press, 2002)

47. Becker, J., **Mentoring High Risk Kids** (Hazelden, U.S.A., Johnson Institute, 1994)

48. Palmour, J., **Mentoring for Masculine Leadership** *in* **Wingspan: Inside The Men's Movement** Harding, C. (ed.) (New York, St. Martins Press, 1992) p. 25

49. Ibid.

50. Ibid.

51. Ibid., p. 29

52. Op. cit., Moore & Gillette, 1990, p. 61

53. Dortch, T., **The Miracles of Mentoring: How to Encourage and Lead Future Generations** (New York, Broadway Books, 2000)

54. Op. cit., Palmour, pp. 22 & 23

55. See also: Taylor, A. and Bressler, J., **Mentoring Across Generations: Partnerships For Positive Youth Development** (New York, Klumer Academic/Plenum Press, in press)

56. West, B., **Submission To The National Museum of Australia: Review of Exhibitions and Public Programs** (South Australia, Flinders University, Department of Sociology, date unknown).

57. Ward, R., **The Australian Legend** (Melbourne, Melbourne University Press, 1966) p. 1

58. Ibid.

59. Ibid.

60. Ibid.

61. Ibid.

62. Australia Bureau of Statistics. Available online – http://www.abs.gov.au/ausstats/abs@.nsf/lookup/NT0001768A

63. Op. cit., Ward, R., 1966

64. Marshall, H., **Introduction To Some Key Themes in Australian Society** (Australia, RMIT University, 2002)

65. Op. cit., Ward, R., 1966

66. Op. cit., Marshall, H., 2002

67. Op. cit., Ward, R., 1966

68. Ibid.

69. Crotty, M., **Making The Australian Male: middle class masculinity 1870 – 1920** (Melbourne, Melbourne University Press, 2001) p. 227

70. Ibid., p.229

71. Ibid., pp. 230 & 231

72. Ibid., p. 233

73. **Gender Equity in Health, a statement of the NSW Health Department** (NSW, NSW Health Department, 2000)

74. **Men and Relationships Program** (Commonwealth Department of Family and Community Services), and, **National Forum on Men and Family Relationships** [carrying the slogans: *valuing men/valuing relationships*] (sponsored by Commonwealth Department of Family and Community Services, October 2004)

75. **Boys in School and Society, a research paper** (Australian Council for Educational Research, Victoria, 2002)

76. West, P., **Giving Boys a Ray of Hope: Masculinity and Education**, a discussion paper for the Gender Equity Taskforce (Australia, University of Western Sydney, 1995)

77. Green, M., **The Next Goal: to make shared parenting the normal parenting style in all families, both separated and intact** (Australia, 2001) Available online – fathersafterdivorce.com

78. Fatherhood Foundation. See website and media release – www.fathersonline.org

79. Kimmel, M., **The Politics of Manhood: Profeminist Men Respond to the Mythopoetic Men's Movement (and Mythopoetic Leaders Answer)** (U.S.A., Temple University Press, 1995)

80. See: Australian Government Department of Family and Community Services, **Mentor Marketplace** Available online –facs.gov.au/internet/facsinternet.ns f/content/mentor_marketplace.htm

81. For an example of a male affirmative mentoring program for young males see: Regional Health Services Program, **Manhood in the Making, mentoring program proposal**. Available online – rhsprogram@saugov.sa.gov.au

82. An excellent example of a Men's Shed Project is the Port Augusta Men's Shed, which has been successful in sustaining a broad range of services and activities. Contact P.O Box 2243, Port Augusta, 5700, online at mensshed@centralonline.com.au

83. Ashfield, J., **The Making of a Man: Recovering masculinity and manhood in the light of reason** (Australia, Peacock Publications, 2004)

84. Op. cit., **Boys in School and Society**, 2002

85. Op. cit., West, P., **Giving Boys A Ray Of Hope**, 1995

86. Ibid.

87. Op. cit., **Boys in School and Society**, 2002

88. Stephen Toon, who conducts these and other programs for men and boys, can be contacted via email – toon@chariot.net.au

89. Ibid.

90. Ian Lillico conducts **Boys Forward** seminars for parents and teachers, in an endeavour to improve teaching methodology and behaviour management, and achieve better learning and psychosocial outcomes for boys. See:
http://www.boysforward.com/04/index.htm

www.ingramcontent.com/pod-product-compliance
Lightning Source LLC
Chambersburg PA
CBHW062208270326

41930CB00009B/1685